# BELONGING ALWAYS

## Reflections on Uniqueness

Philip Mooney

LOYOLA UNIVERSITY PRESS

Loyola University Press
3441 North Ashland Avenue
Chicago, Illinois 60657

*60206925*

Quotations from *Wind, Sand and Stars,* by Antoine de Saint-
Exupéry, copyright 1939 by Reynal & Hitchcock, Inc. Reprinted
by permission of Harcourt Brace Jovanovich, Inc. From *Flight to
Arras* by Antoine de Saint-Exupéry, copyright 1942 by Reynal &
Hitchcock, Inc. Reprinted by permission of Harcourt Brace
Jovanovich, Inc. From *The Little Prince* by Antoine de Saint-
Exupéry, copyright 1943, 1971 by Harcourt Brace Jovanovich,
Inc. Reprinted by permission of the publisher.

Quotations from *Freedom in the Modern World, Reason and Emotion,
Self as Agent*, and *Persons in Relation* by John Macmurray are
reprinted with permission of Faber & Faber, Ltd. Quotations
from other works of John Macmurray are reprinted with
permission of The John Macmurray Trust of Edinburgh,
Scotland.

Library of Congress Cataloging in Publication Data
Mooney, Philip, 1926-
Belonging Always.

Bibliography: p. 173
1. Friendship. 2. Love. 3. Saint-Exupéry, Antoine de,
1900-1944. 4. Macmurray, John, 1891-1976. 5. Mooney,
Philip, 1926-      . I. Title.
BJ1533.F8M66  1987        177'.6       87-2066
ISBN 0-8294-0540-2

Design by C. L. Tornatore

*You*
*—You alone—*
*will have the stars*
*as no one else has them*

—Saint-Exupéry

# Contents

# Preface

Our basic human longing is to belong. Yet the appropriate symbols for the special bonds we form in the time of our living do not come ready-made, precisely because of our uniqueness as persons. This is why we are especially grateful to those rare writers whose close-focused insights and arresting way with words capture the arching significance of "establishing ties" for each of us in turn. This book appreciatively draws upon two such authors, Antoine de Saint-Exupéry and John Macmurray.

The first-named was a French pioneer aviator whose *Wind, Sand and Stars* still stands as the classic for the air age. The other was a Scottish philosopher whose long career as educator stretched from Balliol College in the late twenties (when Evelyn Waugh's *Brideshead Revisited* group gathered at Oxford) to the rostrum of Saint Giles Cathedral in Edinburgh on that last Sunday in November 1963, when the world mourned the fallen President John F. Kennedy. Over those four intervening decades, John Macmurray was to be selected for the major lectureships in religion in the English-speaking world: the Deems Lectures at New York University in 1936, the Terry Lectures at Yale University in 1936, the Dunning Lectures at Queen's University of Kingston, Ontario in 1949, the Gifford

Lectures at the University of Glasgow in 1953 and again in 1954, and the Forwood Lectures at the University of Liverpool in 1960. However, he is best known for his double series of radio talks over the BBC in the early thirties that remained in print for over fifty years under the title of *Freedom in the Modern World*. These were delivered during his tenure as the Grote Professor of the Philosophy of Mind and Logic at the University of London. At the end of World War II, John Macmurray left this post to become professor of moral philosophy at the University of Edinburgh, where he would remain until his retirement.

Saint-Exupéry and Macmurray never met, though in their writings they shared the same key interest in the preeminent value of friendship. Their biographies do cross, however, at the French town of Arras in the Somme region. John Macmurray was awarded the Military Cross for valor there as a Cameron Highlander in World War I. Saint-Exupéry was honored with the *Croix de Guerre* for bravery in air action over Arras on May 22, 1940 during the battle for France.

The French pilot did not survive the war; he was lost on a reconnaissance mission over southern France on the feast of the soldier-saint Loyola, July 31, 1944. That same day, in 1976, John Macmurray's widow, Betty, interred the remains of the kind old Scot in the Quaker cemetery at Jordans, Bucks—just a few paces from William Penn's own marker. John's wife lies buried beside him there now, and I hold their friendship in fond memory. There is no gravesite for St-Ex. But I did visit the house near Northport, Long Island where he wrote *The Little Prince*. The occupant at the time had had the good sense to adorn his writing den with a rug in design of a rose—Saint-Exupéry's symbol for the beloved—"You become responsible forever...for your rose."

*Philip Mooney*
September 26, 1986

# ONE

## *There Will Never Be Another You*

There's an old standard song whose key line is: "There will never be another You." Whether this is meant to suggest elation or relief, I don't recall. But either way, the lyric focuses upon what is most significant about each of us as persons: each of us is *unique*!

In these computerized times, however, this uniqueness of ours becomes obscured, flattened down to the size of our I.D. card that we need to cash a check. We can no longer just tell the teller who we are. No, our identity nowadays is registered as a Social Security number or as a credit rating. We adults can handle this bureaucratic shearing, but it really bothers when our beloved daughter's special worth is thrown into shadow by an IQ percentile or SAT score. (The fact that the testing procedures that come up with the mark for my child are themselves subject to wide error is an early affront to her personal dignity.)

1

Our children, bless them, are less prone to being reduced to a statistic than we adults. Their retort to these metallic, key-punched estimates is a personalized T-shirt or tote-bag. How Eric Gill, the late British architect and bookplate maker, would have loved our young. In one of his last comments on our times, he mused, "Good Lord! The thing was a mystery and we measured it."[1] And even we adults preserve our identity with monogram neck chains and initialed wristbands. And this is as it should be. Since earliest biblical times when Abraham was divinely signatured as father-to-be of many nations, our name has stood for our unique identity. As Anna Maria Alberghetti wistfully rhapsodized in the musical, *Carnival*: "In Mira, every-one knows my name." Home is where you don't need an I.D. You're known there by name!

Our family name bespeaks the glorious tradition of our ethnic origins and the ancestral line into which we were born. With instinctive sure-sightedness, the Hispanic people preserve the fine custom of including the mother's side in the child's full name. Dark-eyed Elena Maria Moreno y Robles, for instance, is enshrined within the heritage of both her parents by her very name.

But it is her given name that catches the limelight: Elena. In giving the child her special name, her parents acclaim, "There will never be another You!" Within the winding lineage of the Moreno-Robles branches that bridged the ocean from Spain to Cuba, there is this golden moment when daughter Elena appears upon the scene. And down through the corridors of all former and future history, there will never be another to take her place. There have been and will be other daughters named Elena, but no other daughter born of these parents at this particular instant in God's caring providence.

To underscore the God-given dignity and *noblesse* of the newborn child, European people often prefer to name the baby for the saint on or near whose feast he or she is born. The birthday of Wolfgang Amadeus Mozart, Western culture's preeminent musical genius, falls on January 27th. So his father Leopold saw to it that his son's first two initials were J.C., because his boy had come into the world on the ancient feast of

John Chrysostom. This is Mozart's name day; just as the September feast of Saint Helen is little Elena's. Antoine Marie Roger Jean-Baptiste de Saint-Exupéry, born in June of 1900, kept the feast of Anthony of Padua as his name day. This little litany reveals how Europeans often make more of their name day than of their birthday. This tradition is likely connected with the Christian practice of introducing the infant into the family of God with his or her baptismal (Christian) name. Even Mary's Son was brought into the covenanted people of God eight days after birth when he was given his name, Jesus.

This centuries-old attention to naming the child is quiet affidavit that the little one's singular worth is God-given. No matter that we don't attend church or synagogue; we still sense that our own irreplaceable quality cannot be fully accounted for by even the most advanced biochemical DNA read-out. Given our "druthers," we favor Isaiah's description, "Even these may forget, yet I will not forget you. Behold, I have graven you in the palms of my hands" (Is 49:15–16). It is so much more reassuring to know that our uniqueness comes of our being the concern of a personal God rather than from random molecular cross-thatching. Of course, we gladly allow genetic charting for our chin-set as the obvious hand-me-down from parental chromosomes; but not quite—for our *uniqueness*! Even the identical twin in the Doublemint commercial holds out for her *own* identity.

This is not to resurrect those ancient squabbles between scientist and theologian. We simply *know* that there is something non-xeroxed about our uniqueness that has us squirm at the scientific brief, but all rest easy in the biblical description. Ironically, it may be Albert Camus, hardly a biblical herald, who put his finger on the "why" for this preference of ours: "But, I know that something in the world has meaning—man—because he is the only being who demands meaning for himself."[2] There *must* be a meaning to personal uniqueness that transcends mere laboratory formulae that can only *classify*.

This demand for significance reflects a threefold conviction at the deepest level of our being that remains impregnable to all encroachments. The first is that we each have interior worth. The second is that somewhere, someday this inner quality will

3

blossom and find its place in the sun. The final leaf in this triptych of personal faith is that this core worth keeps, even in the face of death itself. Camus's demand for meaning comes back to our sense of the unique worth at the center of our personality. His epigrammatic phrasing sums up the yearning for that personal realization which comes in being true to this inner nobility.

But the responsibility for achieving this rests upon each of us alone. The search for personal fulfillment cannot be delegated. Each person is a unique human being seeking personal realization through responsible choice. Because the significance of our life is in the balance, we vigorously resist any infringement upon our prerogative of choice. This freedom is our own tool for reaching mature growth as persons. Part of the stress we feel, even in a democracy, is the pressure of conflicting duties on the job and obligations in the neighborhood that corner us and inhibit the possibility of making *our own* choice.

Yet when we say that mine is *responsible* choice, we are really saying that society holds me responsible for my choice. The B.F. Skinner school of psychological behaviorism, pushed to the limit, might suggest that the reason why I have become a volunteer fireman is that my mother smoked during pregnancy. But society won't let us so easily transfer fault or credit. If I embezzle the bank's money, I will wind up in the dock. Society holds *me* accountable for the decisions I make and the actions I take. Similarly, when a teenager goes on drugs, even when pressured to do so by his or her circle of friends, the decision is his and becomes part of his history. He, along with the embezzler, may later try to shift the blame to his buddies; but the effort is ultimately futile. However, as Camus remarks, there is more in man to praise than condemn.[3] There is also the plus side. When a truck driver stops (as actually happened) and risks his life to save a Chinese couple from their burning car on busy New Jersey Highway 9, this was *his* choice. All the more dramatic because the car exploded just thirty seconds after the rescue. Asked later why he had taken such a chance, the trucker quietly replied that he had to live with himself. He had been true to his unique spirit—and had made a choice.

4

These are the implications of freedom that require a choice we would rather avoid. But it is precisely in these crises that we discover our grandeur, as did the truck driver. In the movie *Gallant Hours*, Admiral William Halsey fends off a compliment with the remark, "There are no great men; there are only great challenges that ordinary people like you and me are called upon to meet." Such was the teenaged girl at Nazareth who changed history by saying, "Be it done unto me according to thy word" (Lk 1:38), and who, with her betrothed Joseph, carried the embarrassing uncertainty of the grace-given child in her womb. Another teenager from Domremy saved France, crowned the dauphin at Rheims, and was martyred by the combined forces of church and state at the age of nineteen. Mother Church acknowledged Joan's courage and sanctity some seven centuries afterwards, but that late endorsement did not help Joan in living up to her interior responsibility in the face of the ecclesiastical court of French bishops who tried her. She remained true to her spirit in keeping to her choice, amidst the flames that engulfed her, and she expired with the name of Jesus on her lips.

These young women dramatized in their own situations that we humans do not live by a philosophy. For a philosophy can be a tidy theory about the nature of humankind whose practical application we have a way of delegating to the lady down the block. You know, the way we do in church, hoping that our obnoxious neighbor sitting at the end of the pew is paying close attention to what the preacher is saying. Sermons and philosophies make for easy referral. But we do have to live by our choices. We are stuck with them, for better or for worse. I identify with my choice: that is precisely what is meant by responsible choice.

Moreover, I *want* to identify with my choice because it is my own personal well-being that is at stake. In every option I take I identify with the appealing image of the person I envisage I shall become through my choice. This thrust for personal fulfillment and maturity is the hidden nudge behind all my decisions. This alone accounts for the option I take in the face of all the alternatives, good and praiseworthy though they be.

My choice is revealed in my action. John Macmurray saves a

step and insists that choice *is* action: "It does not mean that an action is preceded by a choice; . . . the actual choice is the doing of an action; and action is choice whether or not this preliminary reflection takes place."[4] Our actions mirror the priority of our choices because, by and large, people usually do what they ultimately *want* to do, and they duck the boring cocktail parties they cannot abide. When a husband pleads that he had intended to bring his wife carnations for their fourteenth anniversary, but that the florist was closed by the time his bowling league wound up, the excuse is a bit wilted. The husband is really saying that bowling was more important to him than making sure he got the flowers. The man, to be sure, was straddling—as a good many of us do from time to time. But the tale is still the same: the actions we take are the choices we make.

Our life is a series of "I do's," and these cumulatively shape the person we are becoming and bring us personal happiness or personal frustration. We cannot afford to be reckless in what we do without stunting our human growth and compromising our unique worth. In being true to our inner spirit, we each want to make the appropriate decisions that yield personal realization.

Naturally, we seek the necessary wisdom to make the right turns as we head down the road of life. If certain roads lead to a dead end or off a cliff, better to know this ahead of time. Navigational charts showing hidden rocks save broken hulls. Consequently, we turn to our culture as the reservoir of accumulated wisdom that we can draw upon in making our decisions. Actually, the cultural fonts that provide this practical knowledge of how to get on well in the world come down to a basic three: the home, the school, and the media.

Our parents at home, along with church or synagogue as the extension of the family, are the earliest sources of our wisdom about ourselves, the world we live in, and the happiness we seek. Both deliver a lasting set of images of acceptability which become almost unconscious guidelines for our deliberations and conduct in life. Even later rejection or reshaping of parental, priestly, or rabbinical norms of the "good human" still presume these norms as reference points.

In our pluralistic culture, that child is twice blessed whose family and religious teachers took the trouble to raise him or her in a value system, a religion. Amidst the often confusing cross-currents in his young world, such a child always knows where he or she fits in. The child knows that he belongs and has a place in his world of experience. The Judeo-Christian tradition imparts this by insisting that the child is a son or daughter of the God called Father. Such a God is a constant profile in the window that keeps the youngster's world from becoming completely alien. In their later "sophistication," the teenager or collegian may abandon the practice of their religion or put aside the value system they were so carefully reared in; but their religion is still the key point of reference. As Saint-Exupéry put it, the absence of the prodigal son is a false absence.[5] The boy always knows that he has a home to return to and a father waiting. Mary McCarthy and John O'Hara, for instance, are often referred to as ex-Catholics. But ex-Catholics, at least, know where they've come from. Pity the poor child, raised in no religion, with no overall picture of the personal world and of his or her place within it. He doesn't know where he is from, so he has no porch in all this world to return to.

But we must all leave home at an early age, if only during the day to go to school. The child's first day in school is a milestone in his or her upbringing. It is the beginning of the youngster's pull away from home to venture forth into the larger neighborhood. The town church had once been the local community's center for pioneer, homesteader, and urban immigrant alike. But in contemporary America, with its growing number of non-churchgoers, the local public school has become the neighborhood bastion. Ironically, this swing of the pendulum from church to school as the prevailing influence in setting neighborhood mores has occurred just when our "pluralistic puritanism" has knocked any suggestion of religion out of the classroom. Yet in spite of the court-mandated secularism of our schools, this "value-free" system still molds the child by virtue of the many dedicated teachers in the classrooms. No adult can be value-free, if his or her life has any direction at all. With such concerned teachers in charge, our schools function as the

7

dominant formative influence upon our young people during those critical years between puberty and early adulthood. In this way our high schools and colleges serve as the second source of cultural wisdom in our society.

The very designation of many such institutions as colleges of arts and sciences indicates the two types of knowledge essential for any society. The arts or humanities deal with the fundamental values a culture has considered most worthy for human striving. The sciences, in the main, deal with knowledge of the world as useful. Science, in determining what we know about the world we live in, prompts the technology that harnesses the resources of our world for our service. Our space-age travel between continents in a matter of hours attests to our scientific advancement. The magic of Telstar, that can beam Olympic games from Innsbruck and a royal wedding from England, has provided linkage between different cultures in an informative, pictorial way. The computerized technology that could transport a three-man crew to the moon and back we daily find applied in airline reservation monitors and at the grocery store checkout register.

Yet with all this technological advancement, we still need to have a settled priority of values to know what is more worthwhile doing in the time of our living. This means that, for all our scientific progress, we still need the arts. The various forms of art represent the special worth of each significant creature in our universe. Michelangelo's sculpture of Moses depicts the courage of a valiant leader of an oppressed people; his Pietà, the sorrow and serenity of the bereaved mother; and his Sistine painting of the Last Judgment, the ultimate futility of treachery and sin. His compatriot Giuseppe Verdi returned to these universal themes of strength and weakness, sin and reconciliation in the art of the lyric drama so native to Italy, opera!

Opera itself got its start in the Italian Renaissance with the rediscovery of the ancient dramatic classics of Greece and Rome. Plays like the *Oedipus Rex* of Sophocles have staying power through the centuries because they portray the happy or sad consequences of human *choice*! All the arts symbolize the

8

beauty, nobility, and the intrinsic value of what is worthy of human choice. They also depict what is ignoble and beneath human dignity—what man may, and sometimes does, choose to his ruin.

We have touched upon the main reason why we need the arts, that is, to make us keenly aware of the various intrinsic values which engage our personal choice. John Macmurray suggests that "our sensitiveness to intrinsic values is the measure of our civilization."[6] But the late Scottish philosopher of religion also perceived that "the concentration of interest upon instrumental values involves a growing unawareness of and insensitiveness to intrinsic values."[7] Macmurray saw that we were quite advanced in our technological knowledge of the world, but sadly deficient in our knowledge of the world as value:

> When it is the persistent and universal tendency in any society to concentrate upon the intellect and its training, the result will be a society which amasses power, and with the power the means to the good life, but which has no correspondingly developed capacity for living the good life for which it has amassed the means.[8]

John Macmurray's words, written some fifty years ago, have become something of a prophecy fulfilled as far as higher education in the United States is concerned. In the wake of Sputnik, the first Soviet space shot, our government poured millions of dollars into new science programs for our schools, to the dusty neglect of the arts and humanities. Such an imbalance can only harm a society in the long run since its members need both the wisdom of the world as useful from the sciences and the wisdom of the world as value from the arts.

A culture communicates its technological wisdom through the intellectual symbols of the sciences. It conveys its value wisdom through the aesthetic symbols of the arts. This double symbol system reflects the twofold way of knowing within each human person. The intellectual way of knowing is the classification of all the significant beings in our world of experience according to their *common* characteristics. The aesthetic way of knowing, for its part, is the appreciation of the *unique* value of each significant being in the world of our experience.

It is only through our intellectual way of knowing that we come to know the world as useful for our purposes. The table of contents of a textbook in biology is a model of highly organized information. It becomes one of the early reference works in the education of a medical doctor, who one day will be called upon to furnish the appropriate remedy for a diseased organ. His intellectual way of knowing, with its endless cataloging capability, thrives upon the scientific symbols that become his stock-in-trade as a physician.

Unlike our intellectual way of knowing that can grasp the world only in terms of categories, our aesthetic way of knowing reaches the reality of the individual being in and for himself, herself, itself. For this reason John Macmurray considers this other way of knowing that is part of our rational comprehension of the "other" in our experience to be more "objective" than the intellectual approach of science:

> The artistic attitude alone enables us to come into contact
> with the reality of things, to realize the individuality, the
> value of actual objects, actual people ... Art never has to
> seek objectivity, because it is objective from the beginning.[9]

This *appreciation* of the intrinsic worth of another human in and for himself or herself is an intuition that the total accumulation of a person's scientific knowledge cannot provide. What is called the "bedside manner" of a young doctor in treating a patient arises from his aesthetic way of knowing that the arts and humanities nurture in him rather than from all his years of clinical training and textbook learning.

Because it deals in images of special worth, the aesthetic way of knowing is important for an even more crucial reason. It alone puts us in touch with the world as a spectrum of *unique* values which are essential for freedom as responsible choice. Personal freedom presumes knowledge of the world as a challenging variety of significant "values" available for choice. If this choice is to be made in a profoundly considered way, the critical feature must be an appealing, uplifting image of the person the individual is striving to become.

But each person is *unique*, a unique human thrusting toward, thirsting for realization in this very uniqueness. Consequently, knowledge of the world as a spectrum of these images of *unique* value is the fundamental prerequisite for freedom as responsible choice. The reason, quite simply, is that I identify with the value I choose, and I am unique! The young medical student had identified himself with the emerging image of "physician" as the satisfying value that will bring him realization in his personal uniqueness. Our scientific way of knowing, for all of its computerized efficiency and accuracy in delivering knowledge of the world as useful, is of no avail here. Its categories are common and cannot deal with uniqueness. The most obvious choice that dramatizes the limitations of the scientific approach is the decision to marry one's friend. This is the area that science cannot enter because, to go back to Macmurray, science is not more objective; it is merely impersonal.[10]

John Macmurray's central insight is that my knowledge of others in my world depends upon my personal interest in them. But such spontaneous interest is *emotional*, so that the Celtic professor insists that "emotion is essential to the grasp of reality—of the concrete individual."[11] My supreme interest, naturally, is in my own personal realization; it cannot be otherwise. This interior yearning at the heart of my being is my primordial emotion. The startling implication is that the pivotal choices in my life are not based upon intellectual logic, but upon aesthetic, emotional appraisals of intrinsic value. The deep-down thrust within my spirit seeks an appealing image of personal fulfillment that speaks to my own uniqueness.

My choice comes to rest in the value I choose in contrast with those other values I could have settled upon but did not. Why does one brother go to law school and the second become an automobile mechanic? Their high school vocational counselor may well attribute the divergence to their respective *aptitudes* as indicated by a battery of tests. These certainly are the logical reasons that can be conveniently filed with their high school transcripts. The hitch is that a young man equipped with the requisite talents for high accomplishment in law school may

11

still choose to be under the hood rather than on the bench. Here, mere logic fails of explanation.

Logical reasons are set up to serve everyone down the line. They are common reasons broken down by the statistician into categories, variables, and percentiles. However, we in our individuality beg to differ. None of us is everyone. None of us is common. As Walter Kerr observes in explaining the theme of his book, *The Decline of Pleasure*, "we are after some reassurance that we are not statistics."[12] It is our own uniqueness that makes the difference and has me pick up on something special in the option I take, but which holds no attraction for my brother. Fathers often urge their sons to follow in their footsteps; in doing so they may be disregarding the particular identities of their offspring.

Only my uniqueness can ultimately account for my choices, arising as they do in the "emotional" or "motivational" substratum of my personality. This aesthetical appraisal of value that leads to our decisions is called sensibility. John Macmurray defines sensibility as "feeling determining an image."[13] Taking his cue, we can say that in our crucial decisions our own uniqueness aesthetically perceives a signficant value in our experience of the world even as it reshapes this value into the particular image of the person each of us is inwardly longing to become. The reason why intellectual criteria cannot encompass choice is that choice is an aesthetic process in which each person like an artist forms the authentic image of his or her uniqueness for himself or herself.

This is not a reckless endeavor, any more than Michelangelo was carefree in bringing forth his Moses from the Carrara marble. Nor should this aesthetic rendering of the persons we are be regarded as superficial, any more than Titian's portrait of Emperor Charles V or Holbein's of Chancellor Thomas More are counted less valid than the history book descriptions of these sixteenth-century figures. Macmurray remarks that this aesthetic approach "rests in the object of its choice, stirring only to penetrate deeper into the heart of its reality."[14]

This comprehension of interior value is not a knee-jerk, first-blush emotional reaction. No, it develops from an initial favorable impression of "I like it" to the experience-anchored aesthetic appraisal that "it is good." Personal choice is much too precious to be tossed back and forth on the waves of emotional whimsy. This aesthetic appreciation of unique value that is the basis for choice, though difficult of explanation for not being an intellectual process, is as solid a way of grasping reality as scientific reflection. Macmurray supports its objective validity:

> My feeling must really be for the object itself, and the process must be an effort to know and enjoy the object and not to enjoy myself by means of the object. This is the essence of emotional self-transcendence, or, if you will, emotional 'objectivity.'[15]

The arts in their various forms symbolize for us the significant values that engage human choice and bring happiness or frustration. Doing the arts refines our sensibility and stirs our creative impulse to fashion our own images of what is really delightful, gracious, and beautiful in living, and what is not! To neglect the cultivation of this sensitivity to intrinsic value is to restrict one's capability for full choice through one's own mature consideration of what is of true worth in the experience of living. Passing over this crucial dimension of our education is to leave a vacuum that other agencies are intent upon occupying.

Television has! Since the late forties it has become a new voice in the home. With its "total context" projection of aesthetic imagery in peacock colors and exciting sound, television deluges us and our children with instant sense gratifications that do little to enhance our sensibility. (There have been, of course, notable exceptions in its history from the "Firestone Hour" to "Live from the Met.")

Television has effectively become the most persistent non-parental vehicle of cultural "value symbols," especially with the field now left wide open to it by the ill-considered cutback in the arts and humanities by our institutions of higher education. So many of these are today more accurately colleges of science with

13

arts programs tacked on. For better or for worse, television is well entrenched as the third font of the knowledge of the world which our culture provides.

There is no mistaking the global benefits of television. It has established itself as the catholic, or universal, communications medium, humming to antennae perched on huts and hotels all around the world. It has penetrated our insularity and, literally, opened our eyes to the teeming diversity of cultures in the East and the West. We may shut our door to the outside world, but there plunked in the middle of the living room stands the television set. (Movies were always an *outside* influence: you had to make the effort to get to the movie house—on time for the feature—with sufficient funds. Cable television and rental cassettes, however, are now beginning to bring first-run movies into the home. The days of the movie palaces are numbered.) Since television has much to do with channelling our impressions of our world and enhancing or hindering the keen sensitivity to value needed for choice, its role as "educator" calls for careful scrutiny.

The first and most obvious feature about television in the United States is that it is a commercial enterprise. The "industry" is primarily interested in turning a profit, not in instilling personal values. Its daily listings are designed to attract the greatest potential audience for top-dollar advertising clips. The proven negative effects on the young viewer of the high incidence of violence and sexual license on television programs is "rationalized" by the networks in terms of First Amendment freedom of the press. Between the lines, though, it is not hard to decipher the business rationale for the programming: "Shock appeal sells!" This is the overriding consideration. The detrimental impact of excessively "graphic" episodes upon the behavior patterns of the impressionable young is acknowledged with deep-frowned attention on the part of industry executives. So a few scheduling shifts to later, "adult" hours are made, along with some pruning of near-prurient material to offset criticism from the more vocal PTA groups. This, however, is a side skirmish. The ratings war presides as the chief economic fact of media life. What sells, prevails; and our

14

children are left with hardly better than vulgar fare. Images of their inner nobility do not surface much on the television screen.

A turn of the knob should be a ready solution to the content problem. But the persistent effort of children to get in their daily TV-watching is more than most working parents can check. And who checks the checkers? Mom is hooked on her soap operas with their steady stream of major and minor infidelities. Recall the massive publicity buildup to entice an entire nation to tune in to a certain 1981 episode of the evening serial "Dallas." The "come-on" drummed incessantly in the ads and newspaper columns was "Who shot J.R.?" Millions bit the bait and that particular episode topped the Neilsen ratings in some kind of record. Yet, not a very inspiring commentary on U.S. adult viewing tendencies.

For in the process, violence insinuates itself all the more as an acceptable or, at least, a tolerable dimension in the American fabric of life. Sadly, within a year of that slice of TV drama, a Beatle, a pope, a U.S. president, and an Egyptian president were shot, two fatally. In each instance the TV newscasters rightly made pleas for stricter gun control laws, even as their counterparts in the networks' programming departments were planning further "Dallas"-type shootout episodes. William Shannon, writing in the *New York Times*, reported that "by age fourteen, the ordinary child has been exposed to 11,000 murders on television."[16] Little wonder, then, that a friend of mine, an executive in a New York brokerage firm, no longer has a television set in his home. He is that concerned about the possibly harmful effect it could have upon his growing children.

There is another feature about television that deserves even more caution, especially since, as Shannon notes, "the majority of children watch television three to four hours a day throughout their growing years, and one-quarter of all children watch television more than five hours a day, every day."[17] Television viewing in such regular doses tends to close down the creative imagination. This hazard poses itself in two different ways. First, television keeps us from using our own select words to identify our own experience of the world and of our unique

15

place within it by imposing its own image upon our conscious-ness. As a highly pictorial medium, it determines the associa-tions for the words its announcers use, confining the meaning of "poverty" or "picnic" to the pictures it selects. Thus for many a youngster whose family lacks an outdoor charcoal grill, the word "hamburger" more nearly means either the golden arches of McDonald's or the awning caps of the Burger King hostesses featured in the persistent television advertisements. For the more fortunate, the primary memory trace for the word "hamburger" is an image of Dad in the backyard on the Fourth of July, turning over little mounds of meat with his spatula on an outdoor grill and periodically calling over to the picnic table, "Who wants another hamburg?"

Our creative imagination functions primarily through verbal association with images formed of our own personal experiences. The word both identifies our experience and also becomes the reflective and communicative symbol for the experience. We also begin to feature the world of our future and our part in it in terms of this verbal imagination and the associated impressions relating to our past experiences. Some of these experiences may have been joyful, like watching the acrobats at the circus, and others may have been dismal, like getting lost at the circus! In this way, the words begin to take on emotional connotations that reflect our *appreciation* of the experience as good and desirable or as not so good and not so desirable.

The beauty of book reading in lieu of TV-watching is that a word like "circus" throws open the curtain of memory to enrich the word with our own experiential associations in a way that anchors us more firmly in the world of which we form a part. As our verbal imagination becomes more supple and strong, we do not depend upon TV to tell us who we are, what our experiences are, or how to respond. We carry within our own resources a rich and responsive awareness of the world that is our own confident estimate, not the TV cameraman's or the producer's. The words we use stand for our own experience, not that of the television guru, Norman Lear. Words can now serve to repre-sent the future for ourselves in terms of our own appraisals of what is truly uplifting or sad in human experience, rather than that of the Osmonds or Walter Cronkite or Archie Bunker.

As youngsters, however, we didn't have much of a "go" at the world beyond the corner of our street. So we listened to the experiences of others we trusted, our father, mother, uncle or aunt. We began to link words with the evaluations of our father and mother, so that if they would say "Christian" brightly and with a glow on their faces, we felt that there was something good and worthwhile about being Christian. But when they voiced the words "Red Russia" or "Communist Cuba" with a hush, even a tremor in their throat, we sensed that there was something ominous about living in either country under "totalitarian" rule. In this way also, our verbal imagination gathered its clusters of value associations through conversation with our parents in the context of home, in the context of trust, in the context of those who use words to speak the truth, not to sell products or promote a political platform. But how many an adolescent nowadays is deprived of the wisdom of his father or mother's observations upon the world, the poverty in Latin America and Africa, the troubles in Northern Ireland, the soaring cost of U.S. housing—because of the intrusion of TV talk.

Value judgments on world or local events and problems may come more from Dan Rather than from Dad, if the report is true that a child may watch as much as thirty-five hours of television per week, while only enjoying three minutes of serious conversation with Mother or Dad. The difference between Dad and Dan Rather is that Dad communicates value through the emotional connotations of language. Our father will say that there was a "terrible" explosion of a *Mr. Softee* truck on Wall Street this morning, with over a hundred people injured! Or he will take us back to the bicentennial summer in New York harbor with, "Wasn't Operation Sail on the 4th of July a wonderful sight, with all those tall schooners and frigates sailing through the Narrows?"

By contrast, TV news reporting sheers off the emotional connotations of language. This is the second way in which television can stunt the growth of the creative imagination. It took playwright Neil Simon, one of our best wordsmiths, to point out this inadequacy about television: "'Actor Zero Mostel died today in Philadelphia at the age of 62...' The words came from the early evening television news commentator with no more emotion or feeling than the previous item that the New York Stock Exchange was down six-and-a-half points."[18] This so-called "objective" reporting became particularly chafing during the Tet offensive of the Vietnam War when the daily "body count" of U.S. soldiers who died during those dark days were read off by the telecaster in the same monotone as the Dow Jones industrial figures. The human significance of the lost lives of young Americans killed in a war they were drafted into is at the opposite end of the spectrum in personal value from the report of the day's buying and selling on Wall Street. But the difference in meaning could not be detected through any appropriate overtones in the words spoken. The newsman had stripped away the emotional associations of language that carry the value meanings.

If the commentator's news items were compiled in print journalism, the reader would supply his own value associations for "the death of many young soldiers on the battlefield" in comparison with "the average price of stock shares was down 4%." But the broadcaster's spoken message comes from someone speaking in a conversational mode to an audience with sensibility. Yet he jettisons the value connotations of language in reporting all his newsbriefs at the same level of importance. However, if everything is of equal value, nothing is of special value. Left at that, we could hold nothing sacred, nothing worthy of the commitment whose basis is the appreciation of special value. We would find ourselves at the mercy of those who would dictate our options for us, among whom we might not be surprised to find those who set the editorial policies for the major TV networks.

When the spoken word fails to communicate significant meanings, one of the key ways in which special values are shared and responded to goes by the boards. Avenues to the particular aesthetic image we would identify with are cordoned off. Finding ourselves with an uncultivated sensibility and no overall value system to stand for, we would be all the more subject to those who are eager to impose taste in our time. One of the paradoxes of television is the contrast between the news programs and the documentaries. The anchorman for the evening news, in his noncommittal way of speaking, drains phrases dry of aesthetic significance. Yet the producers of the documentary "specials," whether the subject be the Pentagon or the Children of Northern Ireland, can through the adroit selection of camera angle and zoom lens setting, sprightly color or bleak gray, dashing rhythms or minor chords as musical background, artificially manipulate the aesthetic imagery in a way that may or may not reflect the reality of the particular military or Celtic situation under review.

Since we cannot afford to let our creative imaginations grow fallow and ourselves become shallow, we turn away from the television screen back to the written word. For exhilarating, yet serene images of personal meaning, we return to the literature of our creative authors (or to the spoken word of our playwrights) who are dedicated to communicating enduring values through language laden with the heart-felt resonances of love and fear, dreams and dreads, frustration and fulfillment. We go back to where our parched sensibility can thrive once again in response to the emotional symbols of human worth that these word-artists present.

This may sound like a commercial for the liberal arts. Yet even in our television-saturated times, bookstores do a brisk business and good plays on Broadway, like 1981's *Amadeus*, sell out. People still feel inclined to step out of the everyday to refresh themselves with an author or playwright's finely wrought symbols to deepen their sense of significance in the everyday. The routine of work takes on a new attraction with the reaffirmation of its meaning that the arts can supply.

Charles Lindbergh, whose solo transatlantic flight rang in the space age with its astounding technological advances, acknowledged this need in the human spirit for the restorative that aesthetic symbols bring to even the busiest of individuals:

> Too much or too little activity blinds one to true values and
> to the real beauty of living. To observe, to think, and to

19

write well, one should act only enough to keep his senses sharpened and to avoid that theoretical, impracticable, narrow outlook of the man who never acts at all.[19]

The aviator is suggesting that he favors those articulations of human worth whose "clay" is the *experience* of the person who *acts*. Perhaps this is why he and his wife Anne delighted in the writings of their friend, house guest, and fellow air pioneer, Antoine de Saint-Exupéry. St-Ex was a man of action, as he himself insisted, "The notion of being an on-looker has always been hateful to me. What am I if I am not a participant?"[20] His books are literally fire-tested, in the crucible of firsthand experience—in the blaze of Nazi ack-ack guns hazarding his mission over Arras and at the lonely fire lit near his crashed plane in the vast reaches of the Libyan desert. It was for his book, *Wind, Sand and Stars*, recounting this desert experience that Anne Lindbergh set down her exquisite introduction describing the word-artistry of Saint-Exupéry:

> One feels sometimes that the only great stories are those which are so simple that they are like empty cups for people to fill with their own experience, and drink for their own need, over and over again, through the years. One thinks of the Bible stories, fables, the Greek myths, fairy stories, Homer, and the tragedies of Shakespeare. This ordeal in the desert is a kind of 'empty cup' again and each reader must fill it for his own need.[21]

St-Ex had a way of fashioning such chalices with an almost mystic turn of phrase and with such telling impact that three of his works remain among the top ten consistent bestsellers in France. One is his brief, poignant novel, *Night Flight*, followed by his classic for the air age, *Wind, Sand and Stars*. In this book's sweeping grandeur, the aviator-author had sung a paean to aeronautical technology: "Contrary to the vulgar allusion, it is thanks to the metal, and by virtue of it, that the pilot rediscovers nature...The machine does not isolate man from the great problems of nature but plunges him more deeply into them."[22]

For all its marvel and fascination for St-Ex, modern technology could never be more than instrument; allowing it so much sway had sown misgivings within him: "In the enthusiasm of our rapid mechanical conquests, we have overlooked something: We have perhaps driven men into the service of the machine instead of building machinery for the service of man."[23] Saint-Exupéry's uneasiness about an overreaching technology that could smother other more human values was verified in the ruthless, mechanized onslaught of the Nazi *Wermacht* into Poland that precipitated World War II. Within a year of the publication of *Wind, Sand and Stars*, Antoine de Saint-Exupéry was in the skies over his native land, flying military reconnaissance in a futile effort to fend off the Panzer divisions that would rip France apart in six weeks time. Scientism gone berserk! Writing of this unnerving experience, St-Ex was dismayed at the obtuseness of the barren logic that could be so blind to intrinsic worth: "The pure logician, if no sun draws him forth, remains entangled in his logic."[24]

The sunless Nazi regime had turned technology into a relentless war machine, grinding up anything or anyone who stood in its path. Saint-Exupéry was able to slip out of occupied France and embark for the United States where he hoped he could do his prostrate country more good. His effectiveness was blunted mainly because of partisan bickering among the French expatriates in New York City. But the sojourn did furnish the aviator an opportunity to publish *Flight to Arras* and *Letter to a Hostage*. Above all, this brief respite from war allowed him the chance to compose the little book closest to his heart. He would call it *The Little Prince*. This was to be his finale, the last book published in his lifetime. In *The Little Prince*, St-Ex would develop symbols for the values persons live by and which scientific technology is meant to support rather than to shunt aside.

The author had made this very point in *Wind, Sand and Stars*; but his message had fallen upon closed ears. He had insisted that "the central struggle of mankind has ever been to understand one another, to join together for the common weal, and it is this very thing that the machine helps them to do! It begins by annihilating time and space."[25] But the Nazis were even then deploying "high-tech" tools to annihilate thousands of people who deplored their totalitarian ideology.

Because of this perversion of reason, St-Ex in this new little

21

book would cut across the logical categories that adults routinely resort to and write the work jn the form of a children's story. That way no adult could miss his basic meaning. The illustrations, first sketched upon a cocktail napkin in a Third Avenue restaurant, would be his own creation. In every way St-Ex would adopt the personal approach in highlighting the aesthetic dimensions of human reality. The sway of scientism had reached gale force. St-Ex's little book, written in the fall of 1942 in his Northport, Long Island retreat, was destined to stand sentinel for those basic values of human relationship, family and friendship for which so many thousands of Allied servicemen and women had offered their lives.

Saint-Exupéry was to be one of them. The aging pilot had been able to return to his air group in North Africa late in the war. Flying his last reconnaissance mission over southern France near his birthplace at Lyons, he and his craft disappeared without a trace. The log entry of Air Group 2/33 for July 31, 1944 reads simply: "Pilot did not return."

St-Ex was the most honest of men, one who lived and died for what he believed, who kept sorting and shaping and giving expression to the aesthetic symbols to which he could give his full heart. He had a grand way of putting it: "A rock pile ceases to be a rock pile the moment a single man contemplates it, bearing within him the image of a cathedral."[26] Saint-Exupéry echoes John Macmurray in situating this image-building in the personal interest that is love: "Only love can say what face shall emerge from the clay. Only love can guide man towards that face. Intelligence is valid only as it serves love."[27]

His experience as a pioneer of our space age, his advocacy of the benefits of science for humankind, his profound sensitivity to the hidden grandeur of each person—these credentials qualify Antoine de Saint-Exupéry as a fine, although rare cultural touchstone for those images of uniqueness that attract human choice in our time. *The Little Prince*, St-Ex's own primer of personal values, becomes our "empty cup" through which we can relate the significant instances in our biographies to his open-ended, all-embracing symbols. Antoine de Saint-Exupéry is the word-artist who is there with the pertinent phrase for our own sparkling or desolating occasions when language fails us. The day of our wedding or of Dad's funeral are so beyond the everyday and its routine ways of putting things that we stand almost mute. Saint-Exupéry comes along and captures these, our most personal moments with glistening gems of expression that enshrine the experience in our hearts, for good!

# TWO

## Value Images of the World

There are unplanned events in each of our personal histories that prove to be turning points. Saint-Exupéry would look back to his plane crash in the northern Sahara desert on December 30th, 1935 as the providential pause for reflection that restored a sense of priority to his living. This desert experience that had been the centerpiece for *Wind, Sand and Stars* recurs as St-Ex's point of departure in *The Little Prince*: "I lived my life alone, without anyone that I could really talk to, until I had an accident with my plane in the Desert of Sahara, six years ago."[1]

Before this mishap that St-Ex no longer regarded as happenstance, the aviator had included himself as one of those preoccupied adults that the little prince refers to in the tale: "Men set out on their way in express trains, but they do not know what they are looking for. Then they rush about and get excited, and turn round and round..."[2] This search for real, lasting value is the central theme of the book. The guide is the little prince who details for the airman his impressions of the various worlds he finds people living in and the reasons why he could not remain in those realms.

This quest for the *questa cosa*—meaning: "*This* is the settled, reassuring world image of value for me"—is ours as well as the aviator's. We too are off kilter, if ever so slightly, until we come to rest in the right "world" for us, having discovered and refashioned that special image of personal fulfillment that summons forth our uniqueness. But none of these possible world-images of value is valid if they represent a person only as a solitary individual. As John Macmurray puts it so succinctly, "The primary fact is that part of the world of common experience for each of us is the rest of us."[3] An Adam-world lacking his mate Eve would present a lopsided image of the personal universe.

The world images of unique value that truly reflect our personal realm of existence are composite images, comprising an overall image of the world and of oneself as part of that world. Authentic representations of the world of the personal necessarily include the self and others. In fact, it is the specific kind of association with and the characteristic attitude towards those others sharing our particular circle of personal existence that distinguishes the respective world images.

In the world of the king, the little prince finds that the autocrat treats all other people as subjects. This particular world, the first that the little prince investigates, is the world of order, the world of authority. Now we all welcome the benefits of life in a well-ordered society, where those in charge carry out their mandate and the subordinates obey the rules. The hold that Napoleon had on his troops, to take another instance from this world, was that in following his commands they would march in the wake of his triumphs. Happy the kingdom with the good and sympathetic king, like the Christ for the kingdom of heaven. These are the positive aspects appealing to our unique spirit in this world image of personal value, the world of order under authority.

Early on we learned the plus side of such discipline as instilled by our parents. Our good manners took hold as a

26

matter of obedience to the voice of authority, mostly gentle, but at times seemingly harsh. The long-term blessing arising from this "basic training" is that the good manners and good grooming that are necessary for associating with other people, especially at close quarters, are second nature to us. No one had to remind us as young college graduates to take off our hats when going in for a job interview with IBM. When, at times, we do get rambunctious and cut across the traces, alarm bells go off all along our systems. We know almost instinctively that we cannot disturb order without causing some upset somewhere along the line. (We also know that there are occasions when some such upset is demanded, as when Jesus turned over the shekel tables of the buyers and sellers in the temple.)

We all gravitate to the structure where we each can take our respective place as subject. We depend upon others keeping order, even as they rely upon us to do the same. Keeping to our proper traffic lane allows us and the other commuters to get to work or school on time. We count on the mail being delivered and our home not being broken into while we are away. We are annoyed by the chaos caused by strikes, like the mail strike in Italy when thousands of letters were never delivered—the backlog was so overwhelming that the postal service buried five hundred tons of mail! We are bothered by neighborhood decay that somehow increases the incidence of muggings and break-ins. We feel that by agreeing to live in a certain town in a certain country we have made a pact with one another to live by the rules of that town or nation so that we can all get along with our work, our family's well-being, and even our leisure-time activity. The world of order under authority has its points. None of us can do without it. Order is a pillar of society! In fact, there's a certain security in having decisions for the common good made for us by competent and responsible leaders.

Still in all, simply being subject is not enough for a human, as the little prince dramatizes by making a quick exit from the king's turf. The king was in such a bind: he could only issue commands. Yet without a subordinate "at attention," his edicts would be empty pantomine. He desperately wanted the little prince to stay, but the prince declined. Why is this world of order under authority dissatisfying in the end? The little prince offers the most obvious reason: to kings all people are subjects. The uniqueness of each person is not taken into account. In a regimen of rule and bureaucratic policy, everyone is regarded as the same, though no person is ever the same as another.

Another reason why merely keeping the rules does not make for expansive living is that it tends to mold a lifestyle without risk or personal purpose, one of utter routine. Saint-Exupéry himself furnishes us a commentary on this inadequacy in his *Letter to a Hostage*: "Order for order's sake deprives man of his essential power, that of transforming the world and himself. Life creates order, but order does not create life."[4] The "good citizen" could lead an existence as sterile as that of the legalistic Pharisees whom Jesus found wanting. Gilbert and Sullivan caricature the hollowness of such an individual in a line of patter: "He did nothing, and he did it very well!"[5]

There is, however, a more profound reason why we shy away from the image of "subject" as our identifying value. The words "shy away" are used here advisedly. We are picking up on a shrewd observation by John Macmurray that a sure sign of our not fully adopting an option is the hesitancy of fear:

> Even if we know what we want to do, we may be afraid to do it, and our fear may be a constraint *within* us. So long as the fear is there, we can't act freely. Even if we do what we want to do, we shall have to force ourselves to do it, and then we shall not be doing it spontaneously. Strictly, we shall not be doing what we want to do, since our fear is in itself the indication that we don't altogether want to do it.[6]

What we do out of fear is not our own since presumably, without the projected consequences we fear, we wouldn't be doing it.

Now whenever we follow orders or obey a law simply out of fear of the penalty, we are not really giving allegiance to either the law or the orders. By contrast, the immigrants to the United States from lands of oppression embrace the laws of their new country as gladly as his legions marched with Napoleon in a bygone age. As already noted, adherence to the laws of a country or throwing in our lot with a leader we admire are positive actions. Yet the shadow of punishment under the law is always part of the context in this world of order under authority; the hint of fear is never absent.

Moreover, whether our obedience as subject be fleet-footed or heel-dragging, there is a radical limitation at the core of this value that prevents our giving full heart to it. The defect comes to this, that insofar as I am subject, I am deprived of my prerogative of choice. This capacity at the center of my uniqueness is what I tenaciously protect with the last fiber of my being. We may forego the exercise of this prerogative for the privilege of citizenship or loyalty to a leader. But the reservation remains. When the laws of Hitler's *Reichstag* became unjust, loyal citizens like von Moltke spoke out to object, even at the cost of execution. After Fidel Castro, the charismatic commander of the July 26th revolution in Cuba, betrayed his trust and turned totalitarian in the Soviet mold, thousands of his most devoted comrades fell back upon their basic *responsible* freedom to reject him and fled their homeland.

Oftentimes this pressure against freedom shows itself in inexorable cultural custom. Instance poet Dylan Thomas's plight in not being able to come up with tuition money for his children's schooling. Welsh society (and, more so, our own) had established an unwritten rule that all good fathers must pay for the education of their children, and no one took the trouble to ask why. Could not Dylan have educated his two sons and daughter at home, as Leopold Mozart had son Wolfgang and daughter Nannerl, as Jack Yeats had son William Butler Yeats? Dylan Thomas, whom T.S. Eliot described as the greatest lyric poet of the 20th century, was made to feel guilty for a choice not his own. He was not permitted to determine the criteria of being a good father for himself in the context of his own family.

Such "institutional" order in small-town Wales typifies the way any group can set norms of behavior that constrict freedom. The rules of a church promulgated under pain of excommunication are one dimension of such institutionalism. The saving feature of the Church is that many of its members soften the overbearing posture with a real, active compassion for the little person with whom its founder, Jesus, had identified himself: "Whenever you did it for one of these, the least of my brethren, you did it for me" (Mt 25:40). Unique worth still has a claim on the institutional church.

Another counterweight in the Church is that it is catholic, that is, universal, and therefore open to all comers of any ethnic origin or social station, to saint and sinner alike. Scarred with the memory of the institutional lapses that endorsed the gruesome tactics of an Inquisition, some of whose wooden intransigence carries down to our own day, the Second Vatican Council issued its document, *Gaudium et Spes*, the most pastoral statement ever to emerge from an ecumenical council: "The joy and hope, the grief and fears of the people of this age, especially the poor and the suffering, are also the joy and hope, sorrow and anxieties of this assembly."[7] Mother Church, like the father of the prodigal, keeps a welcome haven ready for our uniqueness, even in the shadow of its institutional towers, built from the ancient and ever uneasy alliance with the Holy Roman Empire.

Dylan Thomas had found no such refuge except at the local pub, no more than could the Celtic colleen excoriated by her I.R.A. Northern Ireland enclave for having given her heart to a British soldier. In their own way, our American adolescents are weighed down by the burden of imposed societal mores in the persistent peer pressure to smoke a joint or test sex.

However it comes across, the imposition of law in the world of order precludes our giving full heart to it. No matter how benign and agreeable the dictate or how cumbersome and disconcerting, it is not a decision of ours. This is what prompts John Macmurray's startling observation that "there is no such thing as a moral law and the idea of obedience is not a moral conception."[8] His few incisive lines supporting this position give the reasons why we cannot completely identify with our role as subject in a world of order and must look elsewhere for the fulfilling image of personal value, as did the little prince:

> So far as my behaviour consists in obedience, I am not free.... Someone or something, not myself, decides what I shall do, and I do it because it has been so decided. In that case, I cannot be responsible for my behaviour. It isn't really mine...But,...a man should be responsible for his own

actions; and therefore he must be free to decide for himself what he shall do. That is why morality cannot consist in obedience. To obey is to try to throw the responsibility for our actions on someone else; and that is to deny our own humanity.[9]

What complicates individual response to the originally well-construed laws and well-intentioned customs of a locale is that they inevitably acquire the force of habit. This institutionalization of the traditions of a group, be it family, town, church, or synagogue, always runs the risk of becoming fossilized in normative lore that has long since lost its significance. Saint-Exupéry's quick sketch depicting the pitfalls of such unscrutinized practice recalls the institutional caricature in Puccini's opera, *Tosca*: "The sacristan of a cathedral, in busying himself too much with the location of the altar furniture, risks forgetting that he is serving God."[10] John Macmurray cues to Saint-Exupéry's critique:

> It is not the outward manifestations of religion which determine whether a society is religious or not. These may be merely parts of its traditional structure which persist through habit or because of their political or economic value and may have no relation to the actual nature of the personal relationships between its members by which it lives as a society.[11]

Ironically, Jesus aroused the ire of the Pharisees in setting aside their narrow interpretation of the "traditions of the fathers" in order to cure a cripple on the Sabbath. The cumulative weight of institutionalized tradition in family, church, school, or neighborhood invariably confronts the young adult as he or she seeks his niche in life through his own choice. John Macmurray brings the needed corrective to such canonizing of tradition for tradition's sake: "When we fall back on order, we are really falling back upon the traditional *feeling*—the feelings of other people."[12] The founder of a family tradition was following his own appreciation of inherent value when he first styled his living in the manner that was emulated by his offspring. His great grandson should not, then, be scorned for relying on his own intuitions of intrinsic human worth—even if

31

it means breaking with family tradition. The descendant's freedom is ever as precious as the patriarch's. Heirs do modify family traditions, even as nations amend their institutions of law and order.

But if an institutionalized government in state, church, or even family council looks upon everyone as the same in the world of law and order, at least the premise is that they be treated as persons. In the world of institutional *organization*, however,—whether it be the New York Yankees or General Motors—the individual member is viewed primarily and too often exclusively in his or her *function*. This is the planet of St-Ex's geographer in which the little prince was to carry out the function of "explorer" in that man's geographic society.

This is the world we are most conscious of as individuals. It is the world where most of us work. It also delineates the "role" for which our schools are geared to train us in what is now called "career education." Macmurray suggests that this "process of education 'forms' the character of the growing child so that the pattern of its habitual life fits the function he is to perform, and so that his vision of the good life for himself is that which society requires."[13]

Any organization conspires to achieve a shared objective through the harmonious, efficient operation of all its members. The magnetic appeal of this world that claims most of our waking hours is the common purpose that draws us into the organization in the first place. A baseball player like Joe DiMaggio or a hockey player like Jean Beliveau were attracted by the double benefit of being able to exercise their athletic skills and at the same time contribute to and participate in their teams' achievement of the world championship in their respective sports. An engineer at Ford Motor Company is similarly provided the opportunity to apply his or her engineering prowess to designing a fuel-efficient engine emitting a minimum of hazardous gases into the atmosphere. The engineer's success in doing his part to meet the corporate goals carries the reward not only of producing a good product for the company but also of enhancing the quality of life for his or her fellow countrymen.

These are the exhilarating motives that attract a member into an organization, beyond the financial considerations that, these days, tend to tarnish even the best-intentioned group enterprise. (Nowhere is this more apparent than on the baseball diamond with its Cartier-like salaries, which range far beyond the annual stipend given to the president of the United States.)

For all his joy in exploring—and he did have a knack for it— the little prince could not remain long in the world of the geographer. We, too, have serious misgivings about binding ourselves too tightly to *any* organization. To borrow an expression often overheard at clothing store mirrors: "It (read: the organization) just isn't me." For all our fitting into the organization in filling our various roles, we are still not completely comfortable in it. Being "function" in an organizational enterprise is not our *identifying* image, even though it wears well and is the way we are known to most people.

The drawback that pulls us up short in this world is that in performing our function our own personal realization is submerged for the good of the group. Organizational priority takes precedence over most personal considerations, except, of course, a death in the immediate family. Ironically, this hazard has become accentuated in our age of the large corporation with branches spread across the country and around the world, all within one day's or at most two days' air travel.

How often a father has had to miss a son's high school drama or athletic performance or a daughter's piano or dance recital because his firm had sent him out of town to do his job for the company. The paradox is that the demands of the company upon one's time become all the more pronounced the higher one climbs on the corporate ladder. A recent conference on women in the marketplace reported that the successful U.S. executive must devote upwards of eighty hours per week to the firm, twice that of the low-rung employee. The entry-level wage earner has a much better chance of being at home when his wife's time comes to give birth to their third child than his divisional manager who has been suddenly dispatched to London to expedite an industrial crisis. An executive finds himself with less leeway than the cleaning lady to be on hand for those spontaneous, tender moments in family living that were the original motive for his going off to work in the first place.

This is the preemptive aspect of organizational encroachment, symbolized in the geographer's refusing the little prince's request to put the picture of his flower on his exploration map. Though the flower is the image of the prince's beloved, there is still no room for personal considerations in the world of the tightly managed organization. The implications of the geographer's narrow point of view are quite sobering. The cold, impersonal machine with its relentless cogs and "bits" has displaced the warm, sensitive interplay of the different members of St. Paul's body of Christ (1 Cor 12) as the dominant model for the modern-day organization. Personalist sociologist Emmanuel Mounier called attention to this turnabout long ago:

> Product of intellectual abstraction and the impersonality of things, it [the machine] accustoms us to ways of feeling, thought and experience that are ready-made and impoverished.[14]

Little wonder, then, that the geographer takes the truths of his data-based geology to be "eternal" and dismisses the prince's beloved flower as "ephemeral." This organizational type is simply out of touch with intrinsic human qualities and, like the computer that is the analog for his perceptions, he simply cannot grasp unique worth. Such obtuseness makes more ominous the threat of exploiting the individual—the basic drawback in this world-image of value. "Industry begins with an abstraction," Mounier explains, "ignoring anything that cannot be utilized...By dint of ignoring, we forget, and by dint of forgetting, we deny!"[15] This concentration upon functional efficiency to the neglect of the growth of the human person comes down to organization for its own sake. It risks making institutional organization an impersonal association, however polite and civil its transactions. (The silent shuffling that occurs in cashing a check at *your* bank is very nearly a mechanical exchange.) This machine-like distancing of the craftsman from the head of his "institution" and even from middle management, digs the moats of anonymity within a firm.

The utilitarian mindset that fosters this sort of noncommittal interaction has an unfortunate spillover effect upon society at large. In its preoccupation with speed and efficiency in order to "minimize" inconvenience, the modern organization creates a climate that subtly shields us from the recognition of human suffering. With our sensitivity more and more anesthetized to the pain and anguish in the human situation, we begin to miss encouraging and ennobling glimpses into the grandeur of those fellow humans who bear their incredible burdens of poverty or physical handicap with serene dignity. John Macmurray alerts us to this particular slick spot in our instant-remedy era:

> In practice, sensitiveness hurts. It is not possible to develop the capacity to see beauty without developing also the capacity to see ugliness, for they are the same capacity. The capacity for joy is also the capacity for pain.
>
> We soon find that any increase in our sensitiveness to what is lovely in the world increases also our capacity for being hurt . . . If we choose to minimize pain we must damp down human sensitiveness, and so limit the sources of possible delight. If we decide to increase our joy in life we can only do it by accepting a heightened sensitiveness to pain. On the whole we seem to have chosen to seek the absence of pain, and as a result we have produced stagnation and crudity.[16]

No one screened himself more assiduously from the shin-scrapes in the course of human living than St-Ex's geographer. His little prince punctures the empty aplomb of this inflated organization man:

> I know a planet where there is a certain red-faced gentleman. He has never smelled a flower. He has never looked at a star. He has never loved anyone. He has never done anything in his life but add up figures. And all day he says over and over, just like you: "I am busy with matters of consequence!" And that makes him swell up with pride. But he is not a man—he is a mushroom.[17]

Even then, in the fall of '42, Saint-Exupéry, like Macmurray, had sensed that we had delivered over far too much of the human enterprise to systems engineers, statisticians, and accountants. Mercifully, the locked-in computer programmer with his error-prone, key-punching aide would arrive on the scene too late to disturb St-Ex's eternal rest. The crux is that for all the marvels of moon-shot technology and its information-banking systems, no one can program his way out of the problem of pain. Philosopher Bernard Lonergan had no solution for the enigma of human misery except one—to admit that the pain is there, that human suffering is unfathomable, and to place one's agony on the cross where Jesus takes it, "blotter"-like (Lonergan's word), into the deepest mystery of all: man's inhumanity to God![18]

The callousness of utilitarianism reached its nadir in the Nazi death camps. This shocking chapter from World War II had been foreshadowed by the Third Reich's round-up and elimination of Germany's own retarded children even before the onset of the war. This is so clinically logical, once one adopts the premise that only the "efficient" may stay on.

Overtones of such coldly "demographic" presumptions seep into some of the pro-abortion statements one hears in the United States today. Is it not, perhaps, our deteriorating sensitivity to intrinsic human worth that accounts for the most affluent nation in the world tolerating over a million abortions per year among its people? The rampant utilitarian ethic of our time comes full circle when, to escape from a social or personal predicament, the mother transfers her pain to her unborn child, permitting lethal assault disguised as surgery upon her own body.

When this brand of utilitarianism infects an organization, business or otherwise, it engenders a wary defensiveness in the membership that is counterproductive in the long run. Exploitation of one's talents for the good of the firm, being passed over for promotion for no apparent reason, or even being dismisssed as inefficient or as a nonconformist who bypasses "company procedures"—these are the anxieties that haunt the corporate environment and surface in the "type-A" stress, alcoholism, or even burnout of many organization managers. The fear of being demoted, fired, or losing out in a company takeover may be peripheral, but it is always part of the corporate context.

The fear of exclusion from the group is not limited to industrial organizations. The rookie professional football player reporting to training camp is ever conscious of the possibility that he may not make the final cut to become a permanent member of the squad. In another context, how often in the past has a black or Hispanic, Oriental or Jewish person felt the cold chill of polite repudiation from a golf club or other local society. Failing a final examination has made more than one college senior feel "out of it" on graduation day, as his classmates file by for their diplomas—without him! And even in a recent World Series game, sports commentators attributed the poor base running of the losing team to the fear of reprisal by the club president, should a runner be thrown out at home plate. General George Patton had a slogan: "Never take counsel of your fears." Yet even the best of professionals are confronted with the unwritten logo on the organizational chart: "Produce or else!"

With the corporation's preoccupation with efficient performance, the member soon gets the drift—that, in the last analysis, he is acceptable only in his function and that his association with others in the group is confined to their respective operations. The full-blooded, self-assured man or woman, however, keeps this anemic image of value at arm's length. The genuine human cannot abide being whittled down to impersonal function and is put off by perfunctory, superficial interaction with others. Always in contact, never in touch; careening toward the oblivion of retirement on polite "Good mornings!"—this is high-gloss living that is pleasant enough but too paltry to nourish a life or fill a heart.

And yet people keep going full-tilt for the organization, "hyped" with the hope of success-in-the-offing and immersed in a taxing schedule that prevents reflection upon what's it all about, anyway. It is a merry-go-round world, and the little prince got away from it just as hurriedly as from the businessman's planet.

That latter port-of-call had cured him of all illusions about the businessman's world of economic enterprise. Everything within this man's orbit had to be a profitable item, or else it was

37

remaindered, traded, or scrapped! Even the stars were "property" to this entrepreneur. He owned them, all five hundred million, with each a line item in his accounting ledger. This world was more leaden for the prince than the larger world of the organization, where there were meaningful vistas beyond the narrow scope of money-making. Here in the world of economic enterprise, there was not the slightest sign to reflect the uniqueness of the person; a star in this universe is no longer the Star of David or the Star of Bethlehem, but it is entered and processed simply at its dollar value.

The little prince squirmed at the desk of this money mogul. If this is how this business type viewed the stars, the same kind of cash-register gaze fell on him. The little prince held the interest of this modern-day J.P. Morgan only as a fund producer. It might be tolerable for baseball players like Reggie Jackson to be considered the "property" of the New York Yankees, but the little prince had no truck with this image of himself as a person.

In the world of the geographer, there was, at least, something positive about his function as an explorer, where the prince could bring his own ingenuity into charting newfound plateaus, mountains, and streams on the maps which bore his peculiar imprint. But there was nothing personal about money-making, nor could the currency note in any way reflect the little prince's uniqueness.

The reason why being a fund producer in the world of economic enterprise is inherently dissatisfying as a world-image of value is precisely because it is impersonal. Common tender simply cannot represent unique worth. If a person possesses one hundred thousand dollars in his bank account, there are a number of ways he could have acquired the sum. If he were part of the Rockefeller clan, he might have inherited it. Or he could have won the money in a state lottery. Or he might have robbed a Brink's car or embezzled the nest egg from his firm. Or, hopefully, he may well have earned every cent of the total. But no matter how the hundred grand was lumped into the account, it is the same bland figure. This dollar-sign symbol in no way reflects the person, his history, or his actions.

In view of this, there is a feeling of regret when we see certain occupations that were once professions being flattened down to jobs for which one takes home pay. Time was when teachers "professed" to serve the community, as did medical doctors. Nowadays, for whatever legitimate reasons, some doctors have become very fee-conscious, and unionized teachers are not allowed to stay after school to help a slow student without financial reimbursement. Everyone loses here: the doctor, the teacher, the patient, the student. The doctor and teacher's calling is dedication to those entrusted to their care. But as Saint-Exupéry points out, there can be no gift unless there is someone to receive it.[19] The modern fee schedule and union scale has slammed down the barrier between doctor and patient, teacher and student, though mercifully not in all cases. Doctor and teacher are thwarted in the money exchange because "those who barter nothing of themselves *become* nothing."[20]

We readily affirm that providing for oneself and one's family is necessary and praiseworthy. Even the need to put away ample funds for retirement, the college education of the children, and prospective projects is responsible and prudent. There is, however, the ever-present danger of the infiltration of greed in our money-making, as Jesus cautioned twenty centuries ago: "Beware of all covetousness; for a man's life does not consist in the abundance of his possessions" (Lk 12:15). This warning is still timely: the third page of the *New York Daily News* chronicles each day the lengths people go to for ill-gotten gain. Dire poverty cannot be the reason for these crimes, in a city set up with so many different agencies to provide for the needy. The implication is unavoidable: our consumer culture takes the opposite tack from Jesus and regards that person's life most highly who enjoys ample wealth. Even Christian institutions of higher learning seek out these financially successful individuals to wine them, dine them, and give them honorary degrees in the hopes of securing a hefty donation.

Money is power. Consequently, political office holders and business executives have constantly to steer a careful course to retain their integrity and still keep their jobs under the pressures of prosperous power brokers. We can appreciate the problem of a U.S. Congressman needing the campaign support of a well-financed special interest lobby whose position on a particular bill before the House goes against the welfare of the district he represents. In carrying out his responsibility to his people in voting against the lobby's wishes, the congressman risks damaging the financial base for his reelection campaign. Far too many of our business and government officials have been caught in the thicket of money lures and have yielded. This is why our nation especially admires the leader who has too much a sense of his or her own personal worth to be bought off with money. This is all the more difficult to achieve in the United States where wealth is not only power but the symbol of success. In France, by contrast, a de Gaulle carries within his person the grandeur and dignity of the de Gaulle heritage, even though he or she be as poor as a churchmouse. He does not have to prove himself or make an impression. His interior worth is assured.

But in the United States we are under a constant cultural prod to "make something" of ourselves; and that usually means to enhance our financial standing. In our democracy where we are all happily born equal, we seem to spend the rest of our lives trying to establish how each of us is distinctly different from the rest. Lacking an inner sense of personal worth, we could easily catch ourselves giving ground to the "in"-people advertisements and point to consumer items as marks of our success. Prestige cars are an obvious example, as we reduce the symbols of our individual worth to what money can buy. So superficial and run-of-the-assembly-line! But we still like to think, and do, that the human significance of the medical doctor far transcends any possible symbolism glancing off the hood of his Mercedes-Benz.

The unavoidable factor, in American society at least, is that money and what money can buy are the dominant symbols of individual accomplishment in the competitive world of economic enterprise. Perhaps this trophy aspect is the taproot of greed—the selfish, *individualistic* grasping that insists: "It's mine!" The expression bothers us when we hear it from ornery children. We wince in dismay when these same children grown to adulthood haggle over a dead parent's bequest. Thank God that such desecration is rare in family living.

Leaving the puzzle of greed aside, money-making is the acknowledged symbol of individual success. The higher the post in an economic venture, the greater the salary. A favorite question interviewers ask of prospective young employees is: "How much money do you expect to be making at the age of thirty-five?" This is just another way of measuring the candidate's competitive desire to move to the upper echelons of his company through energetic marketing and managerial prowess.

It is this *competitive* dimension in the economic enterprise that gives us pause. We all agree that sprightly competition is a healthy experience for growing youngsters because that is the kind of world they will have to face when they leave college for the world of business. Certainly, learning how to work and play with others on a team is a fine preparation for life. But the ballots are still out as to whether win-at-all-cost competition like the professional games on television is an unqualified benefit for the growing boy and girl. For one thing, losing is not quite acceptable in our culture where genteel images of failure are in short supply. There seems to be enough competition in the classroom without turning every schoolyard sport into a game that *must* be won. Competition, like sports themselves, has its place. But when it becomes the controlling drive of a person involved in the world of business, it can prompt serious reservations about that person's priorities and character.

One question occurs: Is getting ahead in the company more important to you than your spouse, your children? Would you be willing to take a cut in pay and give up the chance for advancement in order to spend more time with your family? Another question, this one with a direct moral implication: Would you "do in" a friend to get ahead in the firm? Or put another way, are profits more important to you than persons? These questions confront the dark side of the businessman's planet and his world of competitive individualism.

There was a television drama some years ago about a

41

fortyish senior vice president who had been embezzling hundreds of thousands of dollars from his New York City firm. He was also having an affair with a beautiful young blonde in her late twenties. When his felony was about to be detected, he took the money and his mistress and fled to a West Indian island. There on the veranda with its glorious seascape, we catch up with our wiley executive playing cards with his *amour*. Suddenly the woman flings her cards on the table with livid fury and screams, "First, you cheat your company on your way to the top; then, you cheat on your wife with me as willing accomplice. Now, you're cheating at cards! You can't do anything straight, can you?" This win-no-matter-what individualist had dug his own grave of isolation.

This is the deepest rent in the fragile world of economic enterprise. When a man pushes competitive individualism to the limit, trampling upon friends and betraying loyalties, he will end up alone. Oh, he may reach the upper tier of boardroom power and financial preeminence, but with severed ties strewing the staircase. Jesus' first beatitude "Blessed are the poor in spirit" echoes across the empty throneroom of the man's business empire with neither warming hearth nor caring heart to cut the chill there. Business partnerships do not a friendship make, because the prevailing motif is self-interest.

The spirit of self-sacrifice for another person is absent. The competitive individualist has long since shut down this capacity for sacrifice. The crux is that if you sacrifice for no one, you belong to no one. This is the final fallout from any saving grace for the little prince on this planet. The fund-producer image with its impersonal cash accounting registers no vital significance for his uniqueness. And the competitive individualism of the business enterprise verges upon the Gehenna of total isolation that is the ultimate personal frustration.

Subject, function, money-maker—none of these in their respective worlds of value were symbols of uniqueness with which the little prince could fully identify. However, there was still another world to visit, the world of the aviator whom he was to meet on earth. The aviator was quite alone, attending to the wreckage of his plane, when the little prince came upon him.

The prince was glad to hear a solid *"Bon jour"* in reply to his own "Good morning," after the mountains had simply bounced his greeting back again. The prince delighted in hills, streams, mountains, and sheep. But none of these could respond to his need to communicate. Neither an Alpine peak nor a "baa"-ing lambkin could engage him in conversation.

Only humans could. But, the prince had had little luck in interesting king, geographer, or businessman in personal talk. And even here on earth, there was the aviator preoccupied with fixing his plane as if it were the only matter of consequence. Yet the aviator was so genuine and good-hearted, taking time out to do a child's drawing for the prince, that the prince kept up his effort to form a friendship with him. Eventually the prince did succeed in prying the pilot away from the cowling of his engine long enough to let him in on the wisdom of the fox. (In France, *renard*, the fox is the symbol of practical wisdom, that knowledge that a person of action requires to make a go of life.) The essence of human wisdom that the little prince shared with the aviator was the need to "tame" others, that is, to establish the ties of friendship with them. But to prepare for relationship, the little prince insisted that the aviator literally drop all else. This, Saint-Exupéry did. The little prince had made a direct appeal to the very person of the aviator. And the aviator had responded—as a person!

# THREE

## The World of Friendship

Friendship is mutual. This essential feature is so obvious that it tends to gloss over the mystery of friendship. Friendship cannot be forced or programmed. Friendship cannot be organized nor, in the wisdom of the little prince's fox, is there a "shop anywhere where one can buy friendship"[1] ready-made. Friendship comes by invitation, which, in being tendered with graciousness, sets the other person completely free for spontaneous, open response. The slightest pressure would deprive friendship of its glowing quality of mutual enthusiasm untouched by even the slightest hint of obligation.

Its mutuality makes friendship the one mission in life that we cannot accomplish on our own. To act as lawful subject, functional organization member, or a profitable money-maker falls within our competence because these are *individual* human profiles. But to become the friend of another person depends as much upon that particular other as upon oneself. Therein lies the elusive dimension of friendship: My basic longing as a person is to belong to friend and to family. Yet this personal realization in belonging is up to "You," as John Macmurray insists: "Since the 'You and I' relation constitutes both the 'You' and the 'I' persons, the relation to 'You' is necessary for my personal existence."[2]

This puts a dent in the assumption that there is nothing I cannot achieve with talent, ingenuity, and gumption. Strategies, however, simply do not work in the world of friendship. There can be no play-acting at the threshold of friendship; otherwise sincerity, the pure-hearted center of friendship, is clouded over. Friendship cannot be contrived, despite all the romantic lore surrounding courting customs. The complete openness of friendship cannot abide any masquerading of thoughts and feelings. To be a friend is to be in total communication with "You."

The supreme value of friendship is that in the presence of a friend I can be completely myself. I don't have to watch what I say or put a damper on my actual feelings. No one has expressed this refreshing oasis in human living better than Saint-Exupéry in his *Letter to a Hostage*:

> In your company, I don't have to defend myself, I don't have to plead, I don't have to prove. I find peace as at Tournus. Beyond my inept words, beyond the arguments that can do me in, you consider in me simply Person . . . It is not my words at all, nor my manner that have ever taught you who I am. It is accepting the person I am which makes you, if need be, indulgent towards those mannerisms and those ways of speaking. I know you are willing to take me just as I am. What do I have to do with a friend who judges me . . . My friend, I need you like the mountain-top where one breathes again.[3]

The yearning for friendship springs from the heart of our being. It is the ultimate personal value that fully engages our uniqueness because in being friend to You, I am being true to myself. "To be a friend is to be yourself for another person"[4] —this is John Macmurray's fine definition.

The implication is that I'm not quite myself, not totally, when pursuing individual interests as salesman, storekeeper, mechanic, sports enthusiast, financial wizard, Marine commando. The reason why these admirable careers fall short is that, *in themselves*, they are each roles accommodating individual self-interest. These cooperative ventures, for all their reciprocal benefits, are still not enough, as John Macmurray discerns:

> But we will remain isolated individuals and the cooperation between us, though it may appear to satisfy our need for one another, will not really satisfy *us*. For what we really need is to care for one another, and we are only caring for ourselves. We have achieved society, but not community. We have become associates, but not friends.[5]

Professor Macmurray has plumbed our inner spirit: It is the spirit of care that is unique with each of us. Others can keep order in the neighborhood as well as you. If you land in the hospital and have to suspend your work at the company, another will be embarrassingly quick to take your job as production engineer. Still another will make a bonanza in stock trading in your absence from the floor of the Exchange—the knack of making money is no one's particular preserve. But there is no one who can take your place in your characteristic way of going out to others in interest and in love. This is special to you. Your spirit of care comes forth from your uniqueness appreciating the unique worth of the other, and it brims over in your gift of yourself to that person. And when that other person, warmed by the touch of your concern, responds in his or her characteristic way of expressing care, friendship begins to knit. Both of you, in being true to your respective inner spirits that are your particular way of making the gift of yourself, have initiated the personal realization that is friendship.

You know how, after a friendship has kindled to the radiant, hearthside glow of close belonging, you delight in looking back to that chance occasion when you first met your friend: on a bus to work, in a restaurant, at a dinner party. Paging through *The Little Prince* is like that. It is Saint-Exupéry's cherished keepsake, like an album of favorite photos, in which the aviator fondly retraces those treasured moments with his little friend, like walking to the well or simply looking at the stars, back to that very first early morning encounter. In St-Ex's ear of memory, he could always hear the prince's bell-bright greeting that had transformed the thudding desolation of a desert plane crash into the ringing welcome to *become* himself as a person, at last!

The prince had come to earth looking for a friend. But the one who was thirsting for belonging was the aviator. St-Ex had said as much in *Citadelle*, his long-term meditative work that he never finished. The counsel here is fatherly but with a distinctly autobiographical insistence:

> I wanted to instill within you love for your friend. And, at the same stroke, I instilled within you sadness at not being in the company of your friend, just as he who builds fountains, builds their absence . . . Yet, an absent fountain is still sweeter for one dying of thirst than a world without fountains.[6]

The turning point came in the prince's appeal to the inner spirit of Saint-Exupéry, who still clung stubbornly to the emergency duty demanded of him as pilot. But the little prince would not be put off by any career claim, no matter how pressing. He would not let this good man with bursting readiness for dedication be welded down to the leaden mediocrity of the machine, sole link to survival though it seemed to be. The prince felt so strongly about this time-absorbing diversion of the aviator away from his true potential as a person that in the crunch of the situation he broke into tears. It almost reminds us of Jesus' weeping over Jerusalem, so encrusted with a narrow and rigid Pharisaism—"Would that even today you knew the things that make for peace" (Lk 19:42).

The little prince was anxious to have the aviator attend to the uniqueness of a person, symbolized in the prince's beloved flower. Only in breaking free of the engrossing grip of his function could the pilot perceive the special worth of a person that would draw forth his gift and bless him at last with personal peace in mutual belonging. As urgent as the aviator's task was to fix his plane, it was even more important that he find himself as a person. John Macmurray brings these various strands together into a jewel of philosophical wisdom:

> Only in a fully personal relationship with another person do I find a response at my own level... My self-conscious-ness is my consciousness of myself as a person, and it is only possible in and through my consciousness of a person who is not myself.[7]

And this peace in personal realization transpires only in the action of caring for You.

> Only another person can elicit a total response in action, of such a kind that the self-transcendence of every aspect and element of our nature is expressed and fulfilled. This is the implicit intention of all fellowship—the complete realiza-tion of the self through a complete self-transcendence. If this intention could be realized in an actual instance, the self would 'care for' the other totally.[8]

Saint-Exupéry tenderly describes the delicate moment of conversion when he laid aside his wrenches to care for the little prince: "I had let the tools drop from my hands. Of what moment now was my hammer, my bolt, or thirst or death? On one star, one planet, my planet, the Earth, there was a little prince to be comforted."[9] In letting his own self-security slip for the sake of the prince, the aviator had given of himself and had found all of himself in the bond of friendship. Union in belonging is the personal fulfillment that can come only in our being true to our unique spirit of gift.

This is the exhilarating, serene, threat-free summit in human living that poets, playwrights, and opera composers have put to lyric since Adam crooned to his God-given Eve in the garden of divine blessing. One instance is the delightful scene in Mozart's opera, *The Marriage of Figaro*, when on the eve of her wedding to the renowned valet, Susanna sings out her ecstatic joy, "Who could be as happy as I?" Immediately her betrothed chimes in with "I am," in perfect harmony.

Saint-Exupéry rings a change on Susanna's sentiment in his admission, "I, who like everyone else experience the need of being appreciated, feel completely myself in your presence and I go to you."[10] "Appreciation" is the pivotal notion here because it refers to that particular person who would value our gift. This uncovers the other reason why union in belonging is the

49

ultimate engagement for personal choice: I need You because what I do makes a difference to you. Consequently, the motives of my crucial choices are held in trust by You.

We have arrived at elemental terrain in the human situation, once the trivial has been cleared away. We are in the territory of Samuel Beckett, the playwright, who in his Nobel prize-winning play, *Waiting for Godot*, poses the primordial question about personal existence: When the last person leaves this planet who knows who I am, do I still have an identity? The character Didi was beginning to have terrifying second thoughts about himself because on his lonely acre beneath a barren tree his companion Gogo was losing his grip on things and couldn't be sure they had been together the day before. No one who was in the Sheridan Square Playhouse in New York City of an evening back in the fall of '71 will forget Tom Ewell's utter cry of distress as Didi in pleading with Godot's shepherd boy with this desperate intent: "Tell him that I am here and that he's got to remember!" John Macmurray knows whereof Didi speaks and had, much earlier, done the philosophical spadework for Beckett's probing: "My consciousness is rational or objective because it is a consciousness of someone who is in personal relation to me, and, therefore, knows me and knows that I am I. I have my being in that mutual self-knowledge."[11]

The corollary to this basic insight is even more critical for personal choice: When the last person leaves this planet who cares about what I do and appreciates my unique worth, then I no longer have any reason to get up in the morning. This is the dimension of belonging that made Saint-Exupéry ever grateful for meeting up with the little prince, who assured him, "You will always be my friend."[12] Whatever St-Ex would choose to do down along the days and the years left to him, his actions would always have meaning and significance because of the unfaltering concern of the prince.

In the various worlds that we travel, whether in civil society, functional organization, or money-making enterprise, our dealings with others are too often limited to our roles within those realms. The superficial nature of these associations calls into question the significance of what we do and whether or not we

50

are beloved in our uniqueness. To repeat an earlier datum from immediate experience, we do have a persistent, underlying faith in our unique worth and this inner identity is bolstered by bona fide, unsolicited appreciation. A caring friend summons forth my spirit of gift and sheds fresh luster upon workaday routine. For Saint-Exupéry the supreme moment in his relationship with the little prince that had brought him the personal peace in belonging was their walk to the well to draw water:

> This water was indeed a different thing from ordinary nourishment. Its sweetness was born of the walk under the stars, the song of the pulley, the effort of my arms. It was good for the heart, like a present. When I was a little boy, the lights of the Christmas tree, the music of the Midnight Mass, the tenderness of smiling faces used to make up, so, the radiance of the gifts I received.[13]

This "conversation" in which the pilot and the prince had "turned toward" one another in friendship had evoked in St-Ex memories of Christmas. Role distinctions are cast aside on that holy day as we celebrate belonging with one another. This total sharing prompted John Macmurray to call friendship and family the one "religious" institution "because its unity rests upon personal affection and covers every aspect of personality."[14] The Celtic philosopher could have been speaking Saint-Exupéry's own Christmas sentiments in a further comment: "To be a personal relation, the unity must be such that they can *celebrate* it; that they can say together, 'We belong together, and we are glad of it!'"[15]

The religious dimension of the celebrations of belonging that are special to family and friendship on a birthday or at Christmas is the experiential bridge to God that we will take up further along in our reflections. But it is refreshing to notice how Saint-Exupéry sets his self-transcendent relationship with the little prince in the context of Christmas. For many of us in Western culture, our very notion of belonging reverts to the joys of Christmas at home, school, and church, and we still reserve the day to renew that close-knit sense of friendship, away from the anxieties, scrapes, and letdowns in the competitive worlds where we have to make a living.

In his account the aviator is careful to note that his friendship with the little prince didn't just "happen." No, it was by grace of an invitation from the prince revealing himself to the aviator. The prince had laid the groundwork by imparting to the aviator his wisdom, the practical wisdom of *renard*, the fox, that in establishing the ties of friendship we treat each one as the unique person he or she is. This is the initial step; but the key to close friendship is the secret that the prince confides to the pilot: "It is only with the heart that one can see rightly; what is essential is invisible to the eye."[16]

What is essential about a person is that capacity for love which is unique to each. In opening your inner spirit, your "heart" to me, you reveal yourself as person and myself as being invited to friendship and, therefore, capable of the response of love. John Macmurray describes this reciprocal disclosure of the "essential" side of ourselves in two finely turned paragraphs:

> All knowledge of persons is by revelation. My knowledge of you depends not merely on what I do, but upon what you do; and if you refuse to reveal yourself to me, I cannot know you, however much I may wish to do so. If in your relations with me, you consistently 'put on an act' or 'play a role,' you hide yourself from me. I can never know you as you really are . . .
>
> But we must go deeper than this. The 'I' and the 'You', we have said, are constituted by their relation. Consequently, I know myself only as I reveal myself to you; and you know yourself only in revealing yourself to me. Thus, self-revelation is at the same time self-discovery . . . One can only really know one's friends, and oneself through one's friends, in a mutuality of self-revelation. This self-revelation is, of course, primarily practical, and only secondarily a matter of talk. We sometimes call it 'giving oneself away,' and contrast it with 'keeping oneself to oneself.'[17]

Unless you reveal yourself as loving me, I cannot know myself as your friend. The other human profiles for living, be they subject, function, money-maker, sensualist, I can come to know individually because they are individual images. But I cannot come to know you as friend on my own precisely because

friendship is *mutual*. I can look in the mirror and repeat the mime,
"I am your friend," all the while not facing the issue that
friendship does not work that way. Only You can let me know
that I am your friend. If you refuse my invitation to friendship
after I have revealed my interest in you, then I simply cannot
know you as friend. The revelation of 'You' is the way to the
knowledge of friendship, and this revelation needs to be
reciprocal. It cannot be pried open because our inner spirit will
not be straitened. We reveal ourselves only to those whom we
would love, and, like love, this disclosure of our deep-down
dreams and hidden longings is spontaneous and pressure-free.
Above all, this opening of my heart to you and of yours to me is
not at all pragmatic, as crystallized in the crowning gem of
wisdom from the little prince's fox: "It is the time you have
wasted upon your rose that makes your rose so important...
You are responsible for your rose."[18] The utilitarian perspective
has no place in friendship because it would blur the open-
hearted sincerity of mutual revelation and reciprocal gift.

"It is the time you have wasted upon your rose that makes
your rose so important"—no other line in Saint-Exupéry's
grand parable of what it is to be a person has caught my notice as
much as this has. The words have an artless way of riveting
attention upon their meaning, that the grandeur of a personal
relationship lies precisely in its non-utilitarian quality; that my
devotion to a friend, son, daughter, or parent has nothing at all
to do with what they can *do* for me. After all, another would do
just as well if the doing were the basis for my interest. What you
and I love in our friend is that unique, precious, unspeakable,
vibrant, still-center of personal spirit for which there is no
replacement in all this world. Saint-Exupéry's remark raises a
host of images of selfless devotion, but the one that stands out
for me is the silhouette figure of Charles de Gaulle strolling
arm-on-shoulder with his retarded daughter Anne after a heavy
day's work at the presidential palace. How priceless this child,
soothing away the furrows of worry from the brow of the
towering statesman.

To appreciate my friend's special quality, I, like de Gaulle,
have to step away from the swirl of the daily round of

appointments and take on a perspective that transcends the pragmatic preoccupations of the workaday world. This need to change interior lenses is what St-Ex is driving at in this thoughtful line in *Citadelle*: "Love is, first of all, an exercise of prayer, and prayer, an exercise of silence."[19] This quiet reflection that St-Ex calls for frees us for that profound esteem of our friend's interior worth which is the prelude to love:

> Love is, before all, a listening in silence. To love is to contemplate ... The hour will arrive when what you notice in your beloved is not any particular gesture, nor facial expression, nor favorite phrase, but simply Herself! The time comes when just her name, like prayer, is sufficient because you have nothing to add.[20]

There is no ulterior motive in sincere love for a friend. Possessing the beloved as "treasure" is not love. Nor is delighting in the company of a charming guest, because that could simply be "suiting me fine" with the focus ever on self. Sexual expression in itself is not love, as John Macmurray observes so aptly in the face of media saturation to the contrary:

> Love may or may not include sexual attraction. It may express itself in sexual desire. But sexual desire is not love ... A man and woman may want one another passionately without either loving the other. This is true not merely of sexual desire but of all desires. A man and woman may want one another for all sorts of reasons, not necessarily sexual, and make their mutual want the basis of marriage, without either loving the other. And, I insist, such mutual desire, whether sexual or not, is no basis of a human relationship between them. It is no basis for friendship.[21]

But when, in the prayerful regard of other-centered love, the focus is upon our friend, then cooperation in running a household, relaxation in the refreshing presence of a close friend at a birthday get-together, the sexual expression of dedication to a spouse—all these shared activities are transfigured with endearing and enduring signficance.

Sincerity, again, is the touchstone in personal relationships. If you appreciate your beloved, the "rose" of your heart, then you will be "responsible" to her. This maxim of Saint-Exupéry's is put the other way round by John Macmurray: "In the personal field, appreciation is a blasphemy if it stops at appreciation and refuses communion."[22] These are probably the strongest words ever uttered by the soft-spoken man from Maxwelltown. Their forcefulness, however, is understandable in the light of his conviction that insincerity is the worst deliction in human behaviour: "To tamper with the sincerity of your emotional life is to destroy your inner integrity, to become unreal for yourself and others...There is nothing more destructive of all that is valuable in human life."[23]

French aviator and Scottish philosopher share the point of view that when you treat another as *person*, then you are imaging her in her unique capacity for gift. Your interest in another as a person is, in effect, an invitation to her to express herself as person. However, this featuring of another as person is sincere only if you are receptive, responsive, and responsible to her gift of herself in a way that would weave the bonds of friendship. To extend this invitation through overtures of concern for this person and then "cut out" in not "being there" to *receive* the dew-fresh, flowering gift of the other would be a shameful charade. This kind of "cool" insincerity is the preppy dry rot inherent in the Playboy approach to women. If you invite the loving response of another in all her potential for gift, you too are "responsible for your rose."

This open-hearted sincerity requires even more of you, in staying true to your revelation of friendship to another. If your friendship with her should blossom and take root, there will be a readiness for the commitment to the beloved that St-Ex portrays so eloquently, "What moves me so deeply about the little prince...is his loyalty to a flower—the image of a rose that shines through his whole being like the flame of a lamp, even when he is asleep."[24] Communion is transfigured into belonging through your mutual commitment in the shared identity of closest friendship.

But what if, after the initial acceptance of your offer of friendship, your newfound friend eventually decides to make her commitment of identifying union to someone else. The sincerity of your appreciation for her is now put to the ultimate test. For what you love in your friend is her goodness as person—her gentle, gracious, special way of giving of herself in care. This is what you revealed to her in your original glance of affectionate concern. It was by the grace of your invitation that she realized the precious quality within herself. This interior worth of hers is in no way diminished because she now dedicates her life to someone other than yourself. If your love for her is sincere, it is not conditioned upon her making an identifying commitment to you. Your spontaneous love was the candlelight glow through which she came to know herself as person. Your own maturing love freed her for the gift which could have been tendered to you but which, in the untrammelled sincerity of her own heart, she consecrates to another. Your appreciation for your "rose" and your responsibility to your rose is still blessing for your rose, though you miss the full flower of mutuality with your rose.

This total sincerity in making gift, that all too often does not find permanent realization in the total sharing of enduring friendship, is not easy to sustain. In fact, it dramatizes the fundamental human predicament: My realization as a person rests in mutual relationship with You. Yet you go away in the turnings of my life history: through distance, you move to California or, same difference, you go down the church aisle with someone else; through misunderstanding, you part—I just wasn't sensitive enough to your mood swings; through death— I'm still devastated by the onslaught of the cancer that took you from me.

I long to belong, but this belonging seems ever beyond my confident reach. For even if our communication has matured to such a level that neither distance can disturb nor disagreement disrupt, death still looms to separate us inevitably and to hazard our lasting personal fulfillment. Yet, with Camus-like candor, I insist that our friendship should last because I *last*! This enigma at the very core of our personal universe constitutes a kind of cosmic flare-point, signalling our root need for God. God, for us, is that "constant You" keeping us in belonging beyond the crosscurrents of distance, misunderstanding, and death.

The little prince was Antoine Roger de Saint-Exupéry's "constant You" who anchored him in belonging. Before leaving the planet Earth, his young friend had assured the pilot, "In one of the stars I shall be living."[25] So firm was St-Ex's faith in this continuing relationship with the little prince in spite of the yawning distance between them that his final line in his book looks forward to the prince's return—"Send me word that he has come back."[26] In this desert experience the aviator had confronted the age-old, ever-new problem of separation from a friend, and he had come to a settled insight: "The presence of your friend, who in appearance is far away, can become more real than physical presence. It is the presence of prayer. Never have I loved my home more than in the Sahara."[27]

The crux of the question is, however, that the little prince had taken leave of earth by the avenue of death. Could he still be present to the aviator beyond the chasm of human mortality? The prince's parting solace to the airman was that he would be: "I shall look as if I were dead and that will not be true."[28] We have reached the critical juncture in Saint-Exupéry's parable of personhood. If his account is not to fade away in a flight of sheer fantasy, then the person of the prince has to be firmly planted in the human universe, both feet upon the terrain of world history.

Saint-Exupéry is keenly alert to this integrity of inquiry. He is much too serious about his venture to veer away from the cutting edge of the issue that is the fragility of personal relationship caught inexorably in the pincers of death. Quite simply, Saint-Exupéry rests his case in the real identity of the prince himself, in the "impenetrable mystery of his presence."[29] From his own Christian upbringing at home and his education at the Jesuit school at LeMans and the Marist college at Fribourg, St-Ex was well aware that human history discloses only one person to have survived the grave, Jesus of Nazareth. The glorious cathedrals of his homeland with the priceless portrayals wrought in their stone portals, stained-glass lancets, and wooden choir screens had for centuries stood witness to this abiding truth in Christianity.

The author-aviator, however, was too much the artist to

weigh down his reader with a theological tract on this dogma. This would remand the truth to the musty halls of academic theorizing for which he had little patience. No, he would not impose the burden of argumentative logic—"My one temptation is to yield to the reasons of logic when my spirit is asleep."[30] Rather, his prayerful sensibility kept to the beloved object of his quest and quietly acknowledged that his climactic conversation with the little prince, the supreme celebration of belonging in his lifetime, had reminded him of Christmas and its songs of joy in the midnight Mass. In setting this aura around his prince, Saint-Exupéry would raise our vision as to the prince's true identity.

With this heightened awareness, we discover the clues that Saint-Exupéry carefully sifted into his narrative that would reveal the little prince to be the Christ. The prince first appears on earth under a star in the eastern Mediterranean region—as did the Christ child to the Wise Men of old. And when his hour had come to leave this world, the little prince was sent to his death by the bite of a serpent, the biblical symbol for Satan, the power of darkness, that put Jesus on the cross. The morning following his death, the aviator reports that he "did not find his body at daybreak."[31] Jesus' followers, too, had found his sepulchre empty the next day, prompting G.K. Chesterton's comment, "Our faith is based on something that was not there." Christmas, Calvary, Easter—the three central events in Jesus' life among us are retraced in the story of the prince.

Saint-Exupéry is delicately but deliberately adopting a theological point of view to deal with the human predicament in the biological breakdown that ever shadows personal relationship. And with good reason. When we come to discuss personal existence as precisely *personal*, we have penetrated beyond the data of the biological, psychological, and social sciences to the source of personal spirit. If someone were to object, saying, "You are resorting to religious truths," my response would be, "Well, of course, just as all peoples have done since the beginning of time. What other font of truth would one consult in pursuing the fundamental question of survival in personal relationship?"

If indeed Saint-Exupéry's prince is the divine Son of the Father that Christians believe in, then he is the source of personal spirit who is ever present to me and keeps me in belonging always. Only if St-Ex's prince be this Christ who is humankind's last, best hope for personal union to prevail over death, does his story make cohesive sense in the end. Significantly, just as the New Testament finishes with the words, "Come, Lord Jesus" (Rv 22:20), so does Saint-Exupéry's book conclude on the note of yearning for the return of the prince, his "constant You." In his own deft strokes, the French author has captured the exaltation and hope inherent in the mystery of the Incarnate Son of God as expressed by theologian Karl Rahner. The German Jesuit asserts that for our human longing "no resting-place can be found except in Jesus of Nazareth, over whom the star of God stands, before whom alone one has the courage to bend the knee and weeping happily, to pray: And the Word was made flesh and dwelt among us."[32]

Saint-Exupéry once remarked that a star doesn't measure distance but rather betokens presence by its light in our eyes. The star of the little prince is the final illustration in St-Ex's memorial to his friend. It is the Christian symbol of Emmanuel, God-with-us!

# FOUR

## *Self-Protective Fear and Its Solution*

Our happiest moments are spent in the company of our closest friends. John McCormack, the legendary Irish tenor, caught their warmth in his delicate interpretation of the concluding lyrics of a Thomas Moore song:

> Sweet vale of Avoca, how calm could I rest
> In thy bosom of shade with the friends I love best;
> Where the storms that we feel in this cold world should cease,
> And our hearts—like thy waters—be mingled in peace.

This deep peace in belonging is what the aviator had experienced in the presence of the little prince. We too have known this gentle contentment and can sympathize with Saint-Exupéry's yearning to see his friend again. And even in our secularized times, we do not fault St-Ex for seeking recourse in the religious truths of his Christian heritage to open up some glimmering hope for reunion with his friend. In the separation of death we are thrown back upon the origins of personal spirit, for which there is no exact science. For St-Ex, the radiance of the little prince's presence had left an afterglow which dispersed the despair over human mortality. We Christians also, like the poignant Mary in Michelangelo's Pietà, keep a thread of confidence amidst our tears, that somehow in God's caring providence this break with the beloved whom we lower into the ground will not be final.

This is the lingering anxiety that lurks beneath the surface of our daily pursuits: that the bonds of belonging which we have woven together through so many hours of close sharing with our dearest in the days of our years might dissolve without a trace. This prospect of death is the basis of all human fear. Belonging is our fulfillment as persons; irrevocable isolation from our beloved is the ultimate in human frustration. Therefore fear, like love, is an essential ingredient in our makeup. We "love" to belong, and we "fear" isolation. Yet, as with love, fear has many different turns of meaning.

## Our Fears

There is the "instant alert" kind of fear that has us react to on-the-spot dangers that threaten our health and happiness. When I leap from my front porch to keep my child from darting out into traffic, this manifests fear as a healthy response to immediate peril to my youngster's safety. This same sort of wariness keeps me from walking alone at night in certain sections of the city. This is not being paranoid; those are real knives and real injuries, real guns and real victims that are reported on the evening news. We steer clear of concrete danger. This salutary fear keeps us alert to the real hazards present in a large metropolitan population. This is fear as either spontaneous or considered response to known danger.

Another variation of this wholesome fear urges us to stop and think about what we're doing so that our choices and actions won't be reckless or haphazard. This same careful scrutiny carries over into my responsibility for my children. Because I love my daughter, I am concerned about the company she keeps, the activities she participates in, the career she selects, and the husband she chooses for life. For our children as for ourselves, the future is unknown. Still, we want our sons and daughters to make the best possible decisions for the future, just as we ourselves try to do: What job to accept? Where to live? Whether to marry this person? We want to endow our choices with the best wisdom we can muster because we realize that this life is not a "trial run," and we are anxious that neither parent nor child make a botch of it.

This deliberate caution, with its admitted reservations, is healthy so long as it serves the love of the chosen person or the identifying value that prompted our reflection in the first place. Another benefit in this attentiveness is that by taking thought I am able to make a more considerate gift to You. For it is only in my own self-conscious awareness of the pitfalls to human happiness that I can be sensitive to what your real needs are as a person.

However, this reserve that ponders each option becomes restrictive when it makes a person prone to reject even the necessary risks involved in daily choices and actions. Such debilitating fear gets the upper hand through the false sense of security that declines to act at all and prefers the routine of mediocrity to the resourceful leap towards growth and grandeur as a person. It casts its shadow on the Korean War veteran who stops by his local pub after work each evening for his needed palliative. Deep down, this ex-Marine knows he is meant for greatness because he answered the inner call at age twenty-two when he pulled his wounded battery mate out of the Red Chinese crossfire in the Chongjin ravine. His medals and ribbons are collecting dust now, and what grinds on his inside is that he hasn't been challenged since. The peak moment in his biography occurred more than thirty years ago, and he caves in a little more each day to the crumbling rut of clock-punching. This strain of defensive fear has been taking its toll on him lately. Oh, sure he is relatively comfortable in his "all-bills-paid" situation with his guaranteed monthly check. But he is ever restless because he knows, he *knows* that he is not being true to his interior spirit. If fear can make cowards of us all, its favorite guise of "security" can cheat us out of living our own life, and

63

the daily dram of Old Grandad can blur but never obliterate that gradual falling away from oneself.

This uneasiness doesn't burrow in on the person whose characteristic attitude is taken up with others. In this person's readiness to give himself totally to those entrusted to his care, the routine of wage-earning and duties around the house takes on fresh significance because of those for whom he goes to work each morning. The dear person who receives his gift is the reassuring antidote to any hesitancy about risk-taking. Solicitude for self has vanished in the daily sacrifice for the beloved.

Preoccupation with security is a mask for self-oriented fear. This living on the defensive can be habit-forming, as we begin to protect our "turf" in ever widening circumstances. We catch ourselves biting our lip and not saying what we really feel because we don't want to lose our job. We may have resolved to give up our business position to pursue a career in the arts that would be more to our liking, but we hold back at the last moment for fear of upsetting our family. We compromise with ourselves in order to be "acceptable" to others, forgetting that our friends will understand and that, as for those others, it really doesn't matter. After all, it is our genuine friends who hold in trust the motives behind our actions; what we do makes a difference to our friends.

Your friend would, above all, want you to be true to your inner spirit and to shape the life you will be most enthusiastic about leading. To veer away from the path in life to which you are profoundly attracted merely to keep your standing in the institution or to satisfy the people who have come to rely upon you within the institution, be it family, church, or business, is, for all that, insincerity and a yielding to fear. I, no less than you, cannot give full heart to a particular niche in life when there is an interior signal beckoning me down another road toward greater personal gift. To fence in this yearning in order to conform to the expectations and role-models that others have set for me would be to accede to a weak defensiveness.

When this anxiousness about "acceptance" creeps up on me and ever so subtly taints my habitual outlook, I am vulnerable to letting self-protective fear lock in on me as my characteristic disposition. I can keep on top of this tendency as long as I keep my steady focus upon those particular persons entrusted to my care. Their kind regard for me and their generous thoughtfulness will keep me from turning back upon myself, in sustaining me in the warmth of their relationship. By the grace of their interested presence, I am still other-oriented in spite of the "prudence" and tentativeness that might be hedging me in.

However, the factor that does eventually crystallize self-protective fear as the characteristic disposition in a person is the cumulative impact of dismal past experiences in family or friendship. We all long to belong. And we have been richly blessed if, in our life up to now, we have enjoyed beneficial experiences in relationship. In these supportive encounters, our approaches to others as potential friends will have led, often enough, to close, reassuring ties with those persons. Consequently, our basic outlook will have jelled into a confident, outgoing openness to other people.

However, the person who is laden with the bleak disposition of self-protective fear has not been so fortunate. She, too, had gone out to others for the hoped-for belonging. But she has been let down hard more than once by the pseudo-friends she had trusted. She had given of herself but was repeatedly left in the lurch. The Irish saying, "Once burnt, twice shy" sums up her situation. Blue with the bruises of hurtful past encounters, she isn't so quick to respond to more recent beckonings to friendship. She shies away now from getting too involved with anyone and already is beginning to doubt whether comfortable belonging is ever to be hers. She is frankly skeptical about these latest overtures to friendship from this new acquaintance. She has heard this talk before and it has proved to be charming parlor-talk meant to please but not really meaningful! The upshot is that she finds it exceedingly difficult to trust any new invitations to friendship.

This is the most oppressive burden for the person weighed down with self-protective fear, namely, her mistrust of others. Of all persons, she craves the reassurance of belonging because her previous alliances have been so disillusioning. The former disappointments have so encrusted her basic perspective that she dismisses the fresh "revelation of You" which welcomes her to friendship. This disposition of self-protective fear so tightly engrained within her shields out this new revelation in its mistrust of the newcomer as an unpleasant reminder of those who had led her on in the past.

This skepticism about the sincerity of the invitation to friendship makes realization in belonging all the more unlikely for her. For reciprocal revelation that is the channel to close relationships can only come about in the context of trust. But her fear effectively clogs this open communication and thwarts the possibility of forming or sustaining close ties. This negative attitude will bring on what she least desires, a more dreary isolation. This is the pernicious malady undermining relationships that John Macmurray detects with unfailing accuracy: "The defences we build around our precious selves only serve to isolate us from all we really want. There is no fear more potent than the fear of fear, which is the fear of isolation."[1]

Personal realization is in the balance. This dominant disposition of fear must somehow be surmounted since it not only forestalls the initiation of a friendship but can even pull down a buoyant relationship, should one of the parties succumb to its contagion. The possibility of such "estrangement" intruding even into the happiest of marriages, for instance, can never be totally ruled out. The alarming divorce rate in the United States gives us pause; and though the causes for breakup are many, the mistrust sown by self-protective fear may well be the catalyst in many instances. The essence of marriage and friendship is complete, open, and gracious communication. But this cannot transpire in an atmosphere of doubt and misgiving. All of this builds toward the inescapable conclusion that this self-protective fear is the central problem affecting human relationships. So it is imperative that we discover the root causes for this fear and seek a solution.

## Roots of Self-Protective Fear

Fear of isolation is the underlying anxiety upon which this negative disposition feeds. What is it, then, in the past experience of the person that has dealt such a chilling blow of desolation in a promising relationship that it adversely influences the person's overall attitude toward other people? The specific incidents will vary from person to person, but the factors which foster this self-protectiveness can nearly all be reduced to three main roots: the fear of isolation arising from your disinterest in me, or your rejection of me because of my guilt, or my separation from you because of your death.

The first root has to do with the indifference or simply the walking away of someone you had thought you were very close to. This is the most difficult of the three roots to deal with because you can find no apparent reason within yourself for the other person's fading out of the picture or sudden desertion. We can understand, without excusing, what prompted the "Dear John" letters that too many G.I.'s received in the foxholes of Europe or upon the sands of Iwo Jima: The physical separation had simply become too much for the girl back home. This sad history has been repeated more recently when the missing-in-action serviceman returned home from a North Vietnamese prison to find his wife had changed so drastically, as he had too, that they were no longer at home with one another. The long years apart and the psychological pressures of war and confinement had taken their toll. Here, at least, there are concrete reasons for the falling away from friendship.

The more elusive dimensions of this pervasive fear occur in movies like Neil Simon's *Goodbye Girl* which tells of the depression a young woman suffers whose live-in boyfriend suddenly "ups and leaves" with only a note stuck under the telephone. The girl cannot fathom why he went away without facing her; he simply packed and left. We sense her hurt and sympathize with her looking for some cause for his desertion to make it bearable. She had accommodated herself to his needs and wishes and was as dedicated to him as if they were married. More so, in her own mind, because she had to "cover" for their relationship when talking to her family to save her mother embarrassing explanations. Still in all, the flaw, though possibly not within herself, was lodged in the situation itself.

"Living together" is ripe for disillusion and dissolution because the key element of reciprocal commitment is missing.

Either partner can walk out at any time precisely because it is merely a partnership and not a personal union. In a profound sense there is no lasting bond between them because, in the lack of mutual commitment, there is no sacrifice.

This is the insight Saint-Exupéry opened up for me into the fundamental flaw in "living together," although he was actually speaking about giving his life for his country. The thrust of St-Ex's meaning is that if you "sacrifice" for no one, you belong to no one. The key maxim for personal union is: We belong only to those for whom we make sacrifice.[2] From this standpoint the couple living together do not really belong to one another, for all their insistence to the contrary, because they have never made the sacrifice in a total commitment to one another. So as much as we would like to brighten the spirit of the "goodbye girl," there is a reason for her letdown: She and her boyfriend were living together on the fragile base of noncommitment. (Sacrifice means to hold someone sacred, *sacrum facere*, which implies total dedication!)

Girls like this, and men too, who have been sincere in their allegiance to a friend and then abandoned without notice or regrets wear the scars that foster self-protective fear. The prevailing doubt in their heart is whether their newfound friend will also turn apathetic and opt out with the same nonchalance as the last companion. The shock to her self-image had been numbing: She had given all; she was ready for the commitment to marriage at any time and was silently hoping for that moment. But he had never made the promise of permanent love, though his talk seemed to say so. No wonder she draws back from this new tender of friendship. She is caught betwixt and between. She wants to believe in this quiet, polite, and thoughtful person she has recently met; she wants to in the worst way. But the wounds of the past still ache within her, slowing her up with sober misgivings. She could rush to him on rebound from her sorry alliance, but this would only be another symptom of her dread of being treated half-heartedly in still another "made-for-television" relationship. Though he never frequented the singles bars in New York City, John Macmurray describes her distress accurately:

> We pretend that we are enjoying life by working ourselves
> into a state of excitement. We slap one another on the back
> and call one another by our Christian names to pretend that
> we are really in touch with one another, and to cheat the
> feeling of emptiness and isolation that gnaws at our vitals.
> And the sociability, the energy and activity that we create in
> this way is spurious...It is the expression of our fear of
> being alone, not of our love of being together.[3]

Her doubts about ever reaching a permanent belonging crowd
in on her. Some will say she had set herself up for her letdown in
having her affair. That may or may not be, but her sense of self-
protectiveness is just as acute, no matter what part she had in
bringing it on.

What about those others, the man or woman who has not
opted for "living together," who has proved to be a loyal friend
to another only to have that other strike the relationship and
disappear over the horizon. These quietly noble persons,
because of their devotion to their friend, tend to blame
themselves for the rupture, even though they can give no
reason why. This chill of isolation can also touch the young
person who is just getting to know the "someone" in whose
company he can be completely himself. Invitations are exchanged with enthusiastic frequency. There are a lot of good
times together: Christmas dinners with the family, a New
Year's Eve party, birthday gifts. Then all of a sudden the phone
calls stop cold, lines down. "Has she met someone else?" "Am I
getting too serious?" "Maybe she's not ready to settle down?"
"Have I done something to hurt her?" He wants to call to find
out, but doesn't want to complicate the situation. This kind of
fade-out is not easy to take because there is no apparent cause
for the breakup. He searches his soul repeatedly trying to
discover that failing within himself that could account for her
loss of interest.

The effort is inherently futile because friendship arises in
spontaneous mutual response. Consequently, he can give no
reason for her not wanting to deepen the relationship with
greater sharing. Friendship is not formed in logic! The very
spontaneity that brought the two together in the first place is

what has made her decide not to continue seeing him. He might be tempted to recreate the radiant context of their first meeting. But that would be an attempt to organize friendship, and friendship just doesn't work that way. If I try to "organize" you into a fresh round of dating activities, you may go along with it out of interest in the horse show we will attend together rather than out of interest in me. Cooperative ventures are expressions of love only if the prime focus is upon one another. I may "only have eyes for you," but yours are all admiration for the palominos. Your *spontaneous* interest is no longer in me, though you may go along for the occasion because you don't want to cause hurt.

Similarly, the wife whose husband is spending more and more time at the horse races begins to feel that there's something wrong with her, that there's something missing in their life together, or else he would be home more. So she starts to organize her husband by planning Sunday picnics with the relatives, and she cannot resist nagging him about the time he fritters away at the track. No matter, somehow he'll keep playing the nags all the more. John Macmurray's wise counsel should be stitched in needlepoint and framed for her kitchen:

> What we seek in friendship and love is to be wholly ourselves, in equality and freedom, with another person. And there is nothing we can do about this except to trust, to have faith, and to set our friend free of us. [4]

Whether inside of marriage or out, friendship cannot be pressured nor made a matter of duty. Spontaneity is the motif of friendship because it is the essence of love. A gift exacted is no gift at all!

Consequently, you cannot fault yourself if your dearest friend loses interest in you and goes off to other pursuits. In a real sense, you cannot lose what never existed. If a friend departs without any prior hint of dissatisfaction, our hopes are dashed and our feelings pummelled; but the other person had never really put down the moorings of a relationship. Even when the other has been a friend and inexplicably leaves after long months or perhaps years of sharing, you still should not feel there is something wrong with yourself. No one should feel responsible for the decisions or actions that closest friend, fiancée, or husband of twenty years may take for themselves. You have shown yourself a dedicated friend and cannot indict yourself for the other's desertion. Through your graciousness your friend had blossomed as a person. You too had come out of yourself to become more yourself in the refreshing presence of this particular person. You had hoped that the bond would take hold in the strengthening strands of closer sharing. This is a grace for which we can be grateful when it comes our way, but at no point along the way can we engineer another's response.

The fact remains, however, that the self-protective person who fears the isolation of anticipated disinterest has suffered through too many preludes to friendship without experiencing the follow-up of thoughtful attention which leads to a firm tie. Since she hasn't a clue as to why she has repeatedly been left hanging without further signs of interest and sharing, she is not about to "take the bait" now. To her, the signals clearly read that an enduring relationship just isn't meant to be hers, so there is no sense in her pretending that there will be. There is nothing for her to get either "up tight" or excited about. She will simply pursue her mildly successful career and after-hours macramé and steer clear of future invitations, no matter how promising their appeal. Her deep misgiving, veiled beneath her stunning 5th Avenue demeanor, is whether she is really lovable in her uniqueness. This is the root of the mistrust imbedded by too many would-be friends who turned out to be passing charmers.

A wry expression of bemusement creeps over her face when her co-workers tell her that she is being "emotional" in passing up their Friday night parties. Of course she is! Habitual dispositions take their particular texture from the emotional impact of engaging or distressing interactions with other people over the years. And of this she is certain: All the lunch-table advice of her colleagues will not help at all, for all their good intentions. Her fears will not be allayed by logical remedy, though her intellect does help to clarify what is bothering her. She is quite aware that broken pacts and wilted dreams have

71

made her feel the way she does. But her mental sharpness that makes her competent at work and at home cannot change her closed-in disposition.

She cannot reason herself out of an attitude she did not reason herself into. The random patterns in her biography up until now have formed a cross-quilting of joys and sorrows, with the dark colors of past disappointments dominating. Since her outlook has been shaped by brusque treatment that was emotionally diminishing, only the gentle healing of sincere concern from another can restore her trust. Only steady, uplifting attention from a real friend can begin to undo the inner hurt that had begun to warp her attitude toward all other people. Such tender love must, of course, be *emotional*, the soothing assuagement for a disposition bruised from the insensitivity of others. This genuine care will banish her doubts about belonging and the anxiety she feels about being accepted and loved for herself. Only sincere concern will melt the protectiveness that had fended off all approaches to friendship in her resignation that belonging could not be hers.

The transforming warmth of devoted interest is communicated by *affection*, spontaneous, deeply-felt affection. Since there are no preset formulae or ready-made symbols for what is special about a person, only another person's expression of affection for you can image forth the irreplaceable quality in you that is not found in anyone else in all the world. His affection is, in reality, his unique spirit discerning your unique worth as You. Only affection appreciates You in your uniqueness—and the gifts at Christmas and the birthday roses take on their radiance from the glance of tender love that prompted them. The gentle, unobtrusive gesture of kind regard from the other to you becomes the symbol of your unique worth. Affection both sees and expresses how belovable you are in and for yourself. The warming smile of a sincerely dedicated friend is the glad welcome that uproots the fear of isolation brought on by ill treatment in bitter days gone by.

Yet as salutary and necessary as affection is for setting aside the sense of not-belonging that envelops so many young and not-so-young people in our time, its expression is quite restrained in our American culture. One reason, probably, is that we are slow to express in words what might sound insincere. Our media-saturated age has overworked the language of love in movies, television, and commercial advertising so that those phrases may seem stereotyped and empty on our own lips. The late Eddie Doherty, the veteran reporter for the *Chicago Sun*, recalled that on his wedding day he had wanted to say "I love you" to his bride. His hesitancy was that he had used the same formula with so many former girlfriends in a well-meaning but not fully-committed way. Then, in his moment of total dedication to his identifying friend for life, the words caught in his throat as his heart searched for another way to declare the overwhelming devotion that was welling up within him. Sincerity in affection is so essential that worn-out words may seem to deny our tenderest meaning.

Words of affection can also be stifled by the risk of embarrassment. My affection wants to say "You are special," but using the language of heartfelt sentiment might make you feel ill at ease. "Wanting to tell you, but afraid and shy, I let my golden moment pass me by": these lines from the musical *Carousel* sum up our reluctance to speak our affection, for fear of making our friend blush if she is not quite ready for our halting phrases of interior love.

There is another pressure against showing affection for a friend. This is the "taboo against tenderness" that runs deep in the cultures of Northern Europe and Great Britain and has even left its mark in America. This unspoken prohibition is a remnant of the same puritanical narrowness that placed intransigent principle above merciful sensitivity to the starving family who were being evicted by an unyielding landlord. (His type has been immortalized in agent Boycott, who kept a stiff upper lip as he turned Irish tenant farmers out of their homes to the barren bogside.) This Stoic tendency toward duty at all costs goes back to the Caesars: "humane" considerations must never get in the way of established policy! Emotional response is not to be trusted and must be controlled to fit the demands of proper rational principle.

But the more insidious element in the puritanical attitude is the Manichaean condemnation of the human body as the principal source of evil in humankind. Therefore it proscribes sexual expression and unrestrained human emotions as innately prone to sin. This is the bleak view about the "feeling" side of our nature that infiltrated Christianity through its most famous convert, Augustine of Hippo. This far too influential churchman had carried the traces of his Manichaean, albeit libertine youth into his adopted religion, so much so that he considered sexual pleasure to be concupiscence, the vestige of original sin. This repressive view eclipses the Christian teaching in the Letter to the Ephesians that the union of husband and wife is the symbol of the love of Christ for his Church (Eph 5:25).

Yet so strong was the impact of Augustine's teaching upon Christian mores that even into the twentieth century the union of the spouses was subordinate, in Catholic theology, to the procreation of children as the primary purpose of marriage. This is a page right out of Augustine who, still tainted with his Manichaean bias, insisted that the spouses' sexual union in marriage could only be justified on the "rational" need to bring new sons and daughters of God into the world. Stoic principle here becomes the "saving feature" for marital intimacy, which in the Manichaean mindset would otherwise have been proscribed. What an incredible departure from the message of Ephesians! Yet this mix of Stoic "rationalism" and Manichaean indictment of bodily expression has reached down to our own time in the curious rationale that developed around the Catholic condemnation of contraception. Here again the emphasis was upon the requirement that all conjugal activity be open to the possibility of conception, no matter what the detriment to the conjugal union itself. The implication in this is most disconcerting—a good bit of what has passed for Christian morality down through the centuries was not Christian at all, but a blend of Stoicism and Manichaeanism. Little wonder, then, that under the double contagion of Stoic suspicion about the emotions and the Manichaean censure of all bodily sensation, Christian morality has for centuries been preoccupied with sexual morality at the expense of the charity that Jesus highlighted as the touchstone for his Church.

The sad side effect of all this puritanical repression is that the expression of tender affection was also looked upon with disdain and tolerated, ironically, only in the context of courtship. This prohibition against tenderness disregards the fact that our very first experience of belonging was in the loving embrace of our mother and the affectionate hugging of our proud father. Our need to give and receive affection is primordial. It has been the sign and reassurance in belonging since our earliest days, whereas the sexual expression of love does not even become possible until puberty.

However, the cultural reservations about expressing affection still persist, contrary to the teachings of Jesus and to our own longest memories of welcome to belonging. Yet in spite of the hazards of shyness and cultural conditioning, the solution to the first root of self-protective fear is still the warm, sincere, affectionate smile of a friend. Belonging seems so near because of "Your" spontaneous kindness.

## Guilt

The grim puritanical view of the human condition that could hold suspect even the most intimate manifestations of chaste married love and, in the process, put a damper on the most innocent expressions of affection within the home is all the more ominous when it comes to real sin. If the sense of belonging diminishes when the signs of it surface so seldom, its prospects seem especially threatened by the gloom of guilt. This constitutes the second root of self-protective fear—the anticipated rejection from belonging when the checkered history of one's bad past comes to light.

We cherish the hope of permanent union with our newfound love. Yet our sin, be it a single serious lapse or an entire pattern of blighted conduct, towers behind us casting its shadow upon our dreams for the future. There is no denying that mistakes are part of our biography: we each shape our history by the actions we take, to our joy or regret. And our hidden anxiety is that our "prodigal" chapters, whether in doing drugs or in betraying a friend, may have foreclosed the possibility of our finding personal peace in belonging.

This is a formidable shadow to dispel, particularly in our easy-going age of unbridled freedoms that has, ironically, become an age of *angst*. Walter Kerr underscores the anxiety and guilt that have left their mark much too early on too many of our young:

> The man whom no one calls guilty—no judge on the bench, no priest in the pulpit, no injured wife, no neglected child— now turns in on himself and calls himself guilty. He goes further. Since he has not been called guilty of anything specific, he now feels himself guilty of everything generally. [5]

The psychiatrist's couch has become such a familiar furnishing of brief respite from this affliction that words like "guilt trip" and "superego" have become part of our colloquial pattern of speech. Yet there is such persistent honesty at the center of each individual person that the patient *will* not be talked out of her sense of guilt for all the therapist's tactics. The licensed practitioner may insist that she should not feel guilty about living with her boyfriend or about her midweek trysts with a married friend. But she does feel guilty about it! She is an adult and she had made a pact with God, or her family and friends, as with herself that she would adhere to certain ways of living that were consistent with these loyalties. In violating these norms she has let herself down because her word and identifying values are at stake. Her image of herself is rumpled. But any effective cure for her anxiety and guilt begins with her candid admission, if only to herself, that what she has done is wrong by her own standards. Her psychiatrist had called her activity normal self-expression. She has another name for it—"sin," authentic self-expression though it certainly was. It was her own doing!

For unless the cause for guilt is frankly admitted and addressed, there is no prospect of remedy. Though our secular age tries to ignore the reality of sin, pervasive guilt remains to haunt us. It would be an empty kindness to a person who has done harm to her living to gloss over her misdeeds as if they had not occurred. If a son sets out on a course that runs counter to the moral standards that he shares with his family and closest friends, genuine mercy for him, while offering the opportunity for reconciliation, would still deplore the wrongdoing that has brought him so much misery.

At its essence, sin is a violation of a covenant, and it creates its own isolation in the distancing from friends and a falling away from oneself. If we were simply individuals, presumably we could each set our own moral code. But because our personal realization is in relationship and because so much of our daily activity turns upon our association with others, there must be shared norms of interdependence. The concept of sin flows from the notion of a reciprocal covenant. Sin is a violation of that covenant. When Jesus summed up the whole law in the double command of loving God and loving one's neighbor, he put to rest the premise that each individual establishes his own moral standards. Relationship with others implies a shared vision and a shared living from which a shared norm of action must emerge. Sin, with its individualistic bent, is a betrayal, however slight or serious, of some dimension of a relationship— a betrayal of those to whom I belong. Belonging is what is ultimately placed in jeopardy by sin.

Tracing the lines of this second root of self-protective fear, therefore, involves an acknowledgment that we have broken an interior pact. We have to specify for ourselves what particular violation of our personal code has laid upon us our depressing sense of guilt. Our sincere remorse for our mistake and for the hurt it has inflicted upon others issues in a plea for forgiveness from those we have offended.

Open-hearted forgiveness is the cure for the guilt that saps one's confidence in belonging. A certain young girl's sin had damaged her sense of self-worth so badly that she wondered if she could ever be loved for herself again, especially since she had given up on loving herself. She had "messed up" in college—her carousing in wild "coke" parties and reckless involvement in sexual encounters. She sorely regretted all of this when she finally met the clean-cut man she really admired and loved and could have devoted herself to for a lifetime. At least she thought so until that date when she told him the sad escapades that had marred her early twenties. He didn't say much when she had finished; just a mumbling "We all make mistakes." Yet there was an almost palpable chill slowing the flow of their conversation over the rest of the evening until his ever so polite "good night." She never heard from him again. The unfortunate girl was a modern-day Violetta, who in Verdi's opera *La Traviata* exclaims so desolately, "God can forgive but man remains implacable."

No wonder the girl fears rejection because of her past mistakes. She is in a "Catch-22" situation: To be a friend is to be totally open with you. Yet if I tell you the not-so-admirable details in my life story, you may regard me as unacceptable to yourself or to your family and abandon me. Forgiveness is beyond the girl's control. And when, after telling the dark side of her story, she is dropped by her supposed friend, her anxiety about rejection because of her sin is driven more deeply within her. The unhappy girl has begun to doubt whether she will ever find belonging because she is now not sure if she is forgivable. She has been made to feel this way by the vestiges of a puritanism that judges and excludes. The charade of it is that this "giving her wide berth" is too often exercised in the name of Christianity—a hypocritical affront to the founder who had said, "Let him who is without sin among you be the first to cast a stone at her" (Jn 8:7).

This judgmental attitude that runs counter to Christian mercy and forgiveness infests our society. The "adversary" approach is glaringly familiar in labor-management confrontations and in political campaigns. It has even invaded our schools. This pharisaic self-righteousness exerts its widest influence in those television news reporters who often put the individual they are interviewing "on trial." The subtle influence of such media presentations is to foment a censorious viewpoint at the expense of mercy, forgiveness, and giving the other the benefit of the doubt.

Since the climate of our times is not particularly inclined to forgiveness, it falls to the churches and synagogues to reinstill the spirit of mercy and forgiveness that is at the center of the Judeo-Christian tradition. If the modern-day media have been too prone to pass judgment, the sorry chapter of the Inquisition in the Church's history has lent its very name to the condemnatory proceedings that go counter to everything Jesus stood for. The tendency of certain churchmen to stir up a sense of sin and guilt among their members flies in the face of Jesus' dying words of forgiveness, which words remain enshrined in the Lord's Prayer. This is almost to reimpose the burden of sin which Jesus died to relieve. John Macmurray, who considered Jesus' mission on earth "to save from fear," strikes out at this severe miscarriage of Christianity:

> A great deal of Christianity has actually so perverted the plain teaching of Jesus as to conceive that its first duty was to arouse and deepen in men, by all the means in its power, the sense of guilt. This is, of course, one of the subtlest means of destroying the spontaneity in any individual and making him amenable to the control of others. The whole problem for religion, as Jesus clearly saw, was to reverse the process; and so to create the kind of men who could not be imposed upon by authority through their own sense of guilt, but would spontaneously create from a sense of equality and freedom. His method was to assert the falsity of the sense of guilt, without denying the reality of the occasions which give rise to it . . . So Jesus said to the woman taken in adultery, "Neither do I condemn thee; go and sin no more." So he taught his disciples to pray, "Forgive us our trespasses as we forgive them that trespass against us." . . . So at the end, Jesus prayed for those who crucified him, saying, "Father, forgive them for they know not what they do."[6]

Authentic Christianity insists that we are all forgivable. Moreover, the human kindness that forgives also forgets! Belonging becomes a real possibility for the young girl precisely because her past is put forever behind her, never to be thrown up in her face again. In experiencing deep-reaching forgiveness from a new friend who has heard her out and draws her all the more closely to himself, she is beyond herself (ecstatic) with joy as her mental anguish is washed away for good. Hers is the renewal put to song by the French guitar-priest, Père Duval, about Mary Magdalene: "*Il redonne* un coeur de reine a Madeleine"—He restored the heart of a queen to Magdalene.

The grace of transforming forgiveness can totally dissolve the self-protective fear of rejection because of past guilt. What makes this kind of forgiveness break forth in a person is just as mysterious as spontaneous love in the human heart. There is no explanation for it, other than that of the father to the elder son in Jesus' parable of the Prodigal: "We had to celebrate because your brother was lost and is found" (Lk 15:32). Each of us is meant to belong, and the merciful heart of an all-embracing father or friend restores this bond to the much-buffeted Violetta of our time.

## Death

The exclusion from belonging because of guilt can be a living death. But fortunately for us, forgiveness brings relief from this desolation within our lifetime. There is, however, no similar remedy for the cleavage imposed by biological death. This is the third root of self-protectiveness—the isolation from you in the insurmountable separation from you in your death.

The problem of death is ever with us. Yet because of its incomprehensible quality, we try not to think about it. When it imposes itself in the loss of a friend or spouse or other family member, we ease the ordeal with the appropriate rituals for the deceased. Or in the manner of Irish wakes, we soften the blow with a touch of humor, to imply that somehow death does not have the last word. This Gaelic resiliency in the face of the "grim reaper" springs from that culture's ancient Christian belief in eternal life beyond death. Religious faith comes into play when the ties of relationship are threatened by a fatal disease. Mozart leaned upon his Christian upbringing when he received the sad news that his father was dying. In his letter to Leopold, the son wrote, "I thank my God that He has bestowed on me the good fortune . . . of recognizing death as the *key* to our true blessedness."[7] Western culture's supreme musical genius was supported by firm hope while suffering the loss of the person who was parent, teacher, and manager to him. Poet Sylvia Plath was not so blessed, as her friend, the British critic A. Alvarez discloses. He, "as she herself does in the novel (*The Bell Jar*) . . . traces her pathology to a refusal to accept the father's death from a circulatory ailment when she was eight: 'Now she felt abandoned, enraged and bereaved as purely and defenselessly as she had twenty years before.'"[8]

Our secular age does little to prepare our young people for the death of a loved one. For centuries the Christian faith implanted a sense of eternal belonging into the fundamental outlook of the European. This was proof against the terrible ravages of war and plague that seared the history of the Continent. Then rather abruptly after the First World War, something happened: religious faith fell dormant as scientific secularism ran rampant. The consequence was that in the cataclysm of World War II, when military forces swept Europe by air, land, and sea, and the totalitarian regimes killed additional millions of people in their concentration camps, there was no rampart of belief sufficient to withstand this deluge of death.

From the litter of thousands of families torn apart or destroyed, the dark cloud of nihilism emerged as the almost inevitable aftermath. Saint-Exupéry had vanished in the conflict. His buoyant French eloquence was replaced by an Albert Camus, whose arresting phrases were overly somber and lacked the lilt of faith. There is finely wrought beauty in the prose of Camus, but there is no joy there. He frequently decries the rift in the universe that can allow the death of innocent children, with his stark honesty attracting a wide readership among Sylvia Plath's generation. Nevertheless, his recurring theme of the "absurdity" of death furnished no perspective to help the human spirit cope with mortality. Camus' own sudden end in an auto accident added an ironic footnote to his relentless brooding over the unfathomable puzzle of death—a railway ticket was found in his pocket; he had accepted the offer of a car ride to Paris as an afterthought.

The preeminent American playwright Eugene O'Neill was also bothered by the problem of human death, and he met it head-on in his play *Days Without End.* He dedicated this work to his wife, Carlotta Monterey; significantly so, since his central question in the drama is whether a personal relationship with a spouse can survive biological death and keep "days without end."

A half-century or so earlier Giuseppe Verdi had dealt with this same predicament posed by the death of a loved one. Amidst the turbulence in the plot of *Rigoletto*, the ill-starred court jester shows a glimpse of his gentle side as he mourns the death of his beloved wife. *La Traviata* ends with the expiring heroine vowing that she will look after her dear Alfredo from heaven. Verdi himself had walked the dark corridors of bereavement in his mid-twenties when, three years in succession, he lost his infant son, then his infant daughter, and finally his devoted wife. The father-child relationship comes up often in the Verdi operas, perhaps because their composer never got over the loss of his own children. He would eventually marry again, but he was never again blessed with children. In his art Verdi confronted the problem of this final separation from dear ones with prayer, simple prayer to a God who is present both to the survivors and to those who have gone on ahead in death. A number of his operas conclude with a prayer for reconciliation and personal reunion beyond the rupture of death.

If Verdi responded to the elemental perplexity O'Neill faced in *Days Without End* with the unabashed prayer of faith in eternal life, Antoine de Saint-Exupéry found participation in mutual sacrifice to be the key to belonging beyond death. In flying the daily sorties during those disastrous days during the battle for France in the spring of 1940, St-Ex saw two-thirds of his air group wiped out. The reality of death surrounded him on every side, bearing in on him in the form of Nazi fighter planes, "ack-ack" guns, and malfunctioning French aircraft. However it was in weathering the shock of the death of his fellow pilot, Henri Guillaumet, shot down in the fall of 1940, that Saint-Exupéry arrived at his tranquil viewpoint. The response that the loss of his comrade stirred within him rings like a hymn to belonging:

> When Guillaumet, the best friend I ever had, was killed in the course of duty, there was no need for me to speak of him. We had flown the same airlines. Participated in the building of the same structures. Were of the same substance. Something of me died in him. Guillaumet became one of the companions of my silence. I am part of Guillaumet and Guillaumet is part of me.[9]

Belonging beyond death rests upon prayerful faith for Giuseppe Verdi and participation in mutual sacrifice for Antoine de Saint-Exupéry. We cannot deny their assertions because, appropriately, death puts the problem of belonging beyond the measurements of science. Yet we still search for some grounds for hope that our personal relationships will continue beyond the limits of human mortality. Are there any hints in our daily experience of belonging that could point to the possibility that personal union with the person nearest our hearts can persist and prevail over the closure of death?

The first and most obvious feature in our own living out of friendship is that it does not depend upon the physical presence of our friend. You know that you are closer to your fiancé who is on a business trip to London than you are to the office manager whose desk is uncomfortably close to your own. The ties of belonging span any distance, as St-Ex acclaims in a sublime passage:

> Whether he be absent in a nearby apartment or on the other side of the globe, the difference is not essential. The presence of a friend who in appearance is far away can be more real than a physical presence...Never have fiances been closer to their betrothed than the Breton sailors of the 16th century when they were doubling Cape Horn and keeping watch against a wall of contrary winds. [10]

This image of Saint-Exupéry's took on a profound meaning for me in the impact of the news of my father's death from a heart attack at the relatively young age of forty-six. I was away at college and had that very morning mailed him a note of thanks for photos he had developed, printed, and sent to me a few days earlier. I was summoned from the classroom at mid-morning and given that saddest word. That afternoon of November 4, 1947, I was making the slow journey by train from Cincinnati to Cleveland for his funeral. I had not seen my father since a hot day the preceding August when he did look a bit tired. I had blamed his weariness on the oppressive humidity that can envelop Ohio in the summertime.

Now the insight that St-Ex's image opened up for me is that my father was no less present to me on November 3rd, the day before he died, than he had been on that August day when we had said good-bye for the last time. The implication follows directly: Was my father any less present to me in those two hours after he died and before word had reached me than he had been the day before? If the bond of relationship can transcend distance, could it not conceivably bridge the gap of death too? This is a starting point, at least, for our being able to say that there is something about belonging at the personal level of existence that can prevail over the physical separation of death.

The immediate rejoinder may be that your fiancé, away on business in London, is present to you in *memory*, in cherished reverie. The point is well taken. Our friends, as my father was, are present to us in vivid images kept fondly in our memories! The question, then, comes down to this: Is memory the only way in which an absent friend, parent, or spouse are present to us? Is the sense of belonging merely a trace imprinted upon a specific convolution of our brain? If this is so, then at the death of my father I could no longer be present to him even over the miles, because of the onset of biological dissolution.

Does this shut the file, or are there instances in human interaction that might suggest that the personal bond goes beyond biological memory. The "breakthrough" witness in this matter could be the amnesia victim who in the depths of his spirit gropes to recover a relationship still experienced, though no longer remembered. Ronald Coleman portrayed just such a person in the compelling movie rendition of James Hilton's novel, *Random Harvest*. The central character, Charles Ranier, searches for bits of evidence that would reveal the details of a most intimate relationship whose undercurrents still affect him, though their "who," "where," and "why" ever elude him. Charles Ranier had taken the full blast of a German shell at Arras in 1917. The shock of it had blown away his identification tag, along with any clues to his true identity. It was simply as "Smith" that he ended up in a British soldiers' asylum, through whose unattended gates he had quietly walked on the day of the Armistice. In the general rejoicing he is befriended by a vaudeville actress named Paula. After pulling himself together with the selfless support of Paula, Charles, now Smith, embarks upon a career as a feature writer. On its meager proceeds he marries Paula and they settle into the bliss of a country cottage in Devon. Then comes the important appointment with the Liverpool editor that would separate Paula and Charles for the first time. "Smithy" says good-bye to his Paula and boards the overnight train. "Smithy" never made it to the editorial office. He had been hit by a car on the rainy pavement of a Liverpool street and "came to" as Charles Ranier without his wallet or any strand of memory of his three glorious years with Paula. The nasty blow to the head in the accident had jolted him into awareness of his identity up to the moment of the wartime explosion. He returns home and brings the family business back to crisp prosperity. In the course of achieving notable success in British economic circles, Charles has retained a certain Margaret Hanson as his social secretary, quite unaware that she is his Paula. Through a stroke of providence, Charles is summoned to settle a strike in the town where he had slipped out of the asylum years before. A chance stop at the tobacco store where he had first met Paula becomes the searchlight for Charles that illuminates his path back to his wife and full renewal and celebration of their mutual belonging.

James Hilton would agree with Saint-Exupéry that Charles Ranier was part of the person for whom he had sacrificed. Charles as "Smithy" belonged to Paula and she to him—in spite of his tragic loss of memory. All along Charles had missed her, without knowing quite who she was or where to find her. But the crucial factor was that he could not "miss" what he had never known; or else he would not have longed for the recovery of the relationship. This brings us back to the larger question: Can personal relationship with the beloved persist beyond the predicament of death? Perhaps there is a subtle hint of hope for it woven into the experience of the amnesiac who still feels a strong sense of belonging to a particular person, though his memory fails him. If personal belonging is not completely confined to our biological limitations and its memory imprints, this represents a glimmer of affirmation. For hope of reunion beyond the grave is the only possible solution for the ultimate, unavoidable fear of isolation in the death of the beloved. Saint-

Exupéry's assurance that friendship covers ocean distances and James Hilton's, that it reaches even beyond a tragic loss of memory enhance the transcendent dimension of personal relationship.

And yet this does little to console the sorrowing child, parent, spouse or friend, walled off in the finality of their bereavement. Intimations of the possibility of reunion are not enough for the beloved. Nor did they satisfy Eugene O'Neill, who by his own admission unflinchingly wrestled with the inexorable factor in human mortality—"If ever there was an art for art's sake labor, it was mine in *Days Without End.*"[11]

O'Neill finally concludes that the only solution that presents solid grounds for hope of reunion with a friend beyond death is theological: belief in the risen Christ as the source of personal spirit. Early in the drama O'Neill sets out this position in the counsel of the priest-uncle to the central character, John Loving: "Beyond the love for each other should be the love of God in whose Love yours may find the triumph over death."[12] This message is greeted with skeptical indifference by the nephew until he suffers the agonizing ordeal of the near-death of his wife. At the end of the play, John Loving is on his knees in prayer before God in the church of his childhood with, in O'Neill's stage-direction, "his voice rising exultantly, his eyes on the Crucified."[13] His oppressive fear slips away in the ease of release voiced in his prayer of hope: "Thou art the Way—the Truth—the Resurrection and the Life; and he that believeth in Thy Love, his love shall never die."[14]

In confronting the problem of death, O'Neill did not resort to fantasy or even conjecture. The elemental question was far too crucial in terms of human aspiration. He had written the play for those "who are sensitive enough to feel some spiritual significance in life and love,"[15] as he acknowledges in his letter of thanks to the Theatre Guild who had produced it. To his credit, O'Neill did not dodge the issue or balk at introducing the theological dimension as the one adequate response to the primordial peril in the human situation. His implicit position in the play was that there has been only one instance in the course of human history of a specific person who was born, worked, and died in identifiable places and who, after his execution at the hands of the Romans, rose from the dead and reappeared to his closest friends. If this witness be true and this Jesus, the Christ, is indeed the divine source of personal spirit as he claimed, then the fundamental root for all human anxiety at the impending isolation of death has been irrevocably resolved.

O'Neill does not hedge in presenting this as the sole solution, though he had anticipated the disdain with which the play would be received on Broadway. O'Neill had felt that "whatever its fate, . . . it will be heard by a few of them it was written for . . . and will live for them."[16] One of the disapproving New York critics was the "Great Skeptic," George Jean Nathan. The final irony is that shortly before he died in 1958, Nathan became a Catholic. At his own curtain he embraced the message of the play he had "panned." The stalwart of the critical press had joined the "few" for whom O'Neill had predicted the play would live.

## Perfect Love Overcoming Fear

The final line in the play is "Life laughs with God's love again."[17] This is the peak that O'Neill was building toward throughout the drama, that the touch of divine love completely cuts loose the burden of self-protective fear. This radical solution is the one ray of hope that can disperse the dark clouds of human mortality. This divine love showed itself as tender sympathy when Jesus restored the dead Lazarus to his sorrowing sisters. But its overwhelming manifestation came on the first Easter day when Jesus as the Risen Lord joined the company of his two crestfallen friends walking the lonely road to Emmaus. To the eyes of faith this reunion of the divine Son with ordinary people like you and me becomes the abiding basis of hope for the eventual celebration of belonging beyond death that every bereaved person is desperate for. O'Neill had invoked divine love to overcome this most intractable root of self-protective fear because in the odyssey he had vicariously traveled with the central character of his play he had discovered no other avenue of assurance. This is the totally effective spirit of Love in the personal universe that the First Epistle of John describes: "There is no room for fear in love. Perfect love casts out fear...We love at all because He loved us first" (1 Jn 4:18-19).

The perfect love that banishes the fear imposed by the separation from the beloved in death is also the radical solution for the fear of isolation that results from another's disinterest or another's rejection because of one's sin. It is true that your new friend's sincere concern has broken down the defensive shell put round you by the indifference of a former companion. You rejoice in the sunshine of his affection. Yet you wonder if it can last. Will self-interest begin to blunt his sensitivity to your particular yearnings, as happened with the others? The old song line, "Will you love me in December as you loved me in the May" with a counterpoint in the Beatle refrain, "Will you ever need me, will you ever leave me, when I'm sixty-four" voices your misgivings. The rash of divorces in the United States among couples married twenty years and more underlines your uneasiness as to whether you can be appreciated in your uniqueness by any friend for very long. The radical remedy for this lingering apprehension about your friend's eventually growing tired of you is *constant* sincere care for you just as you are.

The prospect of such constancy is especially dubious in our times when we put so much emphasis upon the externals: financial success in the man, physical attractiveness in the woman, and efficient performance from both. What gets blurred in all this is our own sense of worth, making us wonder if we are lovable in our uniqueness apart from the way we look or how we do our job. The sense of failure that can overshadow a person for not measuring up to the "acceptable" norms reinforces his inner doubt as to whether he can be appreciated for himself.

No one has depicted this down-in-the-mouth forlornness more dramatically than the late Emmett Kelly in his portrayal of the clown Willie. The out-of-work hobo wanders hungry and downcast under the big-top until a child offers him a peanut. Food at last! Willie borrows a sledge hammer from a circus hand to use as a nutcracker. Down comes the hammer; "Doggone!"—to his dismay, Willie's morsel is smashed to smithereens.

Willie notices the jugglers getting applause for their dexterity. So he finds a feather, balances it on his red bubble of a nose, and he too hears the shouts of acclaim. Basking in his unaccustomed success, Willie steps forward for his bow to the audience, only to have his suspenders snap! Applause shifts to guffaws—his embarrassment eclipses Willie's moment in the sun.

But never mind! Willie would retrieve the gold of this special occasion as he tries to sweep the gleaming bits revolving in the spotlight into his dustpan. But the bright circle gets smaller and smaller until it disappears altogether. Willie has come up against the elusiveness of lunch, the elusiveness of success, and the elusiveness of the golden moment—these criteria of human achievement are not to be his.

Still he does not feel that his underlying significance as a person lies in these "perishables" anyway. So he gathers a bunch of red roses for his lady, who is demurely seated in a box at ringside. Shoulders high and with sprightly step, Willie prances forward in his flapping tatters to present his bouquet of devotion. Sadly, he is turned aside, disappointed in love—the tears in his eyes glisten above the unshaven hollows of his cheeks.

Willie could handle failure, if only he were loved for himself. Emmett Kelly had shaped the character of Willie from the shattering experience of his real-life divorce from his first wife, Eva: "After the divorce I became melancholy for long periods and this feeling worked its way inevitably into Kelly, the clown. With my family scattered, I had only the sad-faced hobo, and we became at this time indistinguishable."[18] In his autobiography, Kelly expands his thoughts on why we had let our gaze trail him round the tent and had doubled up in laughter at his fumbling efforts at life and love: "By laughing at me, they really laugh at themselves, and realizing that they have done this gives them a sort of spiritual second wind for going back into the battle."[19]

We, too, have known failure as a bread-winner. We've been "let go," been caught in the crunch of a corporate merger, or been laid off when a plant was shut down. And we have not won

89

the gold medals for high performance in the competitive world that loudly proclaims that winning is "the name of the game." We also may have been hurt when our dearest friend walked away.

We appreciate the antics of Willie because our failures need symbols every bit as much as our successes do. Our pragmatic world, so impatient with inefficiency, has not bothered to devise symbols for the "also-ran." And yet our slips and stumblings are also part of our biographies, and they cry out for representation. Willie has done that for us. The chorus of approval under the big-top melts the layer of isolation that our failures had cast about us. Sad-faced Willie is a universal symbol that reassures us that we are not alone in our defeats, and that others "have been there" too. Our glumness disappears in the ripples of compassionate humor that Willie stirs in our hearts.

Past disappointments are put behind us, all except the persistent need we have to be loved for our own sake by someone who will always care, no matter what. That cannot be dismissed with a tent-laugh. This is why the hobo reaches for home at Christmas. Even the scruffiest, most abandoned vagrant recovers a sense of belonging at the Bethlehem crib.

What is there about this one day of the year that sets aside all discussion of success or failure, of past gaffes, and says, "Come as you are—you are welcome because you belong?" Christmas is a celebration of belonging in which no one is excluded because it is a renewal of the moment when divine Love came into the world in the form of an infant who welcomed poor shepherds and rich Magi alike. Western culture has never let go of this image of belonging and the *constant* concern that the birth of the divine Son of God as the Christchild symbolizes. This is the vein of divine love that is the radical remedy for those who have known the hurt of an initially sincere, open-hearted friend falling away after a time or even after long years of marriage. The interior anguish borne in by the cumulative indifference of those to whom one had devoted a good slice of a lifetime needs the soothing grace of this more-than-human love. Such a person's weary history of repeated letdown by trusted friends has undermined any confidence he or she might have had that anyone can set aside self-interest enough for steady, ongoing, complete devotion to another. The warming light of Christmas dispels this defeatism and puts spring back into his or her step for their pilgrimage through life.

The profound significance of Christmas, beyond the wrappings and the cards, centers upon this child of Mary. Its hidden meaning is that God's Son, who was involved in my personal start—and therefore knows me in my uniqueness for having inspired my identity with his creative touch of love—cared enough for me, just as I am, to share everything with me by being born human like me. This is the underlying reason why everyone feels at home in the shelter of Christmas. Each of us in our own special being, whether our particular history has been mainly "up" or decidedly "down," is linked to this child because of his own initiative. The good news sung to the shepherds by the angels is taken up in the Christmas exaltation of St. Paul, who cried out, "The Son of God . . . loved me and gave himself for me" (Gal 2:20). Christmas celebrates the glad truth that each of us is beloved in our uniqueness always, *always*, because of this breath of divine love that is total, selfless concern. I wonder if this isn't the key to the meaning of Saint-Exupéry's final line in *Wind, Sand and Stars*: "Only the Spirit, if He breathe upon the clay, can create man!"[20]

A further stream of this divine spirit can also freshen the heart of the most hardened criminal. This is what the angel meant when he said that the mission of Mary's son was to save people from their sins.[21] Sin is the focus of Jesus' saving action. In a basic sense, realization in belonging is more threatened by the effects of evil deeds than by the prospect of death. For if in the divine design the veil of death is eventually to be lifted away, access to reunion is still blocked in the desolate conscience of the sinner who has gravely wronged friend, family, or fellow human. The ne'er-do-well is convinced that he has forfeited any claim he may have had upon that glorious fulfillment in personal belonging. He persists in his despairing attitude, even though the friend he has hurt has spoken the gracious words of forgiveness to heal him and their relationship. Yet the man cannot forgive himself. This is the puzzle implanted far beneath the surface of personal interaction that defies easy explanation. However, it may be the very goodness of the friend he has so shabbily treated that he takes to be her blind spot allowing her to overlook his misdeeds. His inner voice says, "You are so good-hearted and so kind in your regard for me that you cannot begin to grasp the real malice of what I did to you. Such evil has no part in you. But if you really understood how bad my action was, you would never exonerate me and take me back."

His friend's forgiveness does not relieve this man's burden of sin because he does not see himself as *forgivable*. There is no help for his situation unless he is assured of absolution from one who knows how bad his sin is and can still forgive. This is no less than an urgent plea for divine mercy. For only the divine Son, as the creative source of his unique personal spirit, can penetrate the dark reaches of his particular guilt. The divine Son can forgive as human representative for the injured friend, because the man's sin involves a violation of an unspoken covenant with God, the origin of personal life and love, to whom he is also responsible. This is the inner plaint expressed by John Loving, O'Neill's central character, before the church crucifix: "O, Son of Man, I am Thou and Thou art I! Why hast Thou forsaken me? O Brother, Who lived and loved and suffered and died with us, Who knoweth the tortured hearts of men, canst Thou not forgive—now—when I surrender all to Thee..."[22]

The *unconditional* forgiveness of the divine Son on Calvary is the radical solution that wipes away the last trace of guilt and erases the fear that could not even trust offers of reconciliation. Remorse can make us feel that our sin is more pernicious than any other and beyond the reach of possible forgiveness. Calvary settled that misunderstanding once and for all. Jesus as God's Son suffered the worst evil that any human can inflict upon another, to take the life of an innocent person; and he could still forgive—"Father, forgive them for they know not what they do" (Lk 23:34) is his prayer for his executioners. That is the profound, perduring significance of Calvary.

The divine Son, who fully plumbs the limits to which the human power for evil can extend and who was himself tortured and done to death, did not falter in his own unlimited capacity for healing love. Promising the repentant thief paradise that very day, God's Son showed that divine mercy prevails over humankind's direst potential for malice. Jesus is the Jewish man who can forgive Hitler, because He is the divine Son. This *unconditional* mercy means that no one of us is beyond the power of God's forgiveness. Magdalene stood at the foot of the cross and the reformed thief was hanging next to Jesus in those last moments of his earthly life, when darkness covered the earth. The total impact of Jesus' death in ridding the world of the oppressive gloom of guilt is radiantly verified in his Easter presence to his friends—the final and lasting dimension of the divine love that first appeared on Christmas night. These three moments in the love of the Incarnate God for us, Christmas, Calvary, and Easter, stand as the *constant* concern, the *unconditional* forgiveness, and the *enduring* hope for reunion beyond death that provide the ultimate dissolution of the three main roots of self-protective fear.

# FIVE

## *Prayer and Divine Presence*

For centuries Western culture has celebrated belonging in
the context of Christmas, Calvary, and Easter to renew our
consciousness that we are not alone, that divine love continues
to permeate the personal universe, and that our fears and
failures do not have the last word. The feast of the Magi was
observed as a holiday in what is now the continental United
States long before Thanksgiving was. The architects of the
Spanish missions in Florida and California worked in the
tradition of the 12th-century French guilds who raised the
vaulted arches of Chartres, Rheims, and Strasbourg, their
brilliant stained glass depicting the central events in the life of
Christ for an illiterate populace. (The Gutenberg Bible was still
three centuries yet to come.) Throughout the ages from
Charlemagne to Churchill, artists like Donatello, della Robbia,
Michelangelo, Murillo, da Vinci, El Greco, Raphael, Rembrandt,
and Rubens have impressed the main lines of the Christian
message upon the European consciousness. In our own age

while Sartre was proclaiming that there was "no exit" from the existential morass left in the wake of the great wars and Camus was struggling, however valiantly, with the "absurd" threats to human well-being, their countryman Georges Roualt kept to his studio, poring over his poignant paintings of the Christ. The heavy black brush strokes outlining the scarred features of the "Man of Sorrows" on trial for his life were the very same face markings Roualt had used for his clowns![1] This was the Expressionist's response to the grim surveyors of war-torn Europe: no human failure or sin or atrocity could close the book on human aspiration because Christ is the "clown," the rejected of mankind, pushed from the scene as a criminal to be executed outside the walls of the "City of Peace!" Jesus' Easter triumph over his own death on Calvary gathers in, "as a hen gathers her brood under her wings" (Lk 13:34), Willie the clown and all the other people tossed upon vacant shores by the waves of disappointment; and he transfigures their ineptness, ridicule, and raggedness into glorious significance. With an assist from Willie, we can let a grin seal our failings and we can put forever behind us our somber biography of sins in the cosmic vision of Roualt's Christ. For after his fall into human mortality on Good Friday, Christ got up again on Easter Sunday to validate his mission in overcoming all fear.

Is this turning to divine love as the radical salvation from fear a case of escapism? Is this solution a real dynamic influence in our everyday human experience? The secularist bias of our age, which is a late arrival in Western culture, is inclined to dismiss that possibility because it does not fit neatly into its categories of observable data. However, we should not be too quick to adopt the scientific mindset to interpret all aspects of our world, as John Macmurray intimates:

> The visionary dreams of the medieval church of a universal empire over the hearts of mankind, purified by obedience and submission, was not so madly irrational as the modern dream of a world made peaceful and happy by obedience to the dictates of scientific thought. The formula of the three persons in one God is sensible and significant when you put it side by side with the meaninglessness of the fundamental formula of scientific faith, that one and one makes two.[2]

We cannot summarily brush off the continuing presence of the divine in human affairs simply because there is no scientific construct to account for the Incarnate Son of God. We shouldn't, after all, expect that science could so provide, any more than the scientist himself can measure the reason why his wife loves him. There is a dimension of reality in our personal relationships that simply cannot be grasped scientifically. For his part, John Macmurray was alert to the signs of God's presence in our personal world because for him, "Jesus linked the love which He manifested . . . with the hidden reality of the world, with the creative center of all things."[3] This reinforces Macmurray's contention that the world of the divine impinges upon our own world and that "what our childishness thinks of as another world, a supernatural world, is merely the reality of this world which is hidden from us by the imperfection of our own sensitiveness!"[4] The Edinburgh professor is echoing the exclamation of his fellow Briton, James Hilton: "We are spies for God, mapping out territory lost to the enemy, when faith was lost!"[5] This religious perspective that detects the workings of the divine in our personal relations insists that the impact of Christmas, Calvary, and Easter is ever available and effective to relieve the depression of the person who is crushed under the burden of fear.

The crucial question, then, looms large: how do we become aware of this hidden dimension in our personal world that will bring us the touch of divine kindness that will free us from crippling fear? There is a single reply to this inquiry, ranging from Paul to Pascal, Origen to O'Neill, Benedict to Bernadette, Anselm to Auden, Anthony of the Desert to Antoine de Saint-Exupéry: prayer! During the darkest days of World War I, when the full force of the Allied crisis pressed down on the shoulders of Marshall Foch, the supreme commander, a carping "hanger-on" complained one morning to Clemenceau that Foch was wasting time praying in a small village chapel near the front. The French premier briefly retorted, "Our cause always goes better after Foch's visit to his church."

The most dyed-in-the-wool agnostic respects the man of prayer because he cannot deny its integrating influence on an individual. Prayer seems to allow a person to be above the fray while he is in the midst of the crossfire. "Contemplative in action" was how someone described Ignatius of Loyola, who "found God in all things and saw all things in God."[6] Men like Loyola and women like Mother Teresa and Joan of Arc seem to have tapped wellsprings of spiritual strength that remain closed to the rest of us. Prayer is a habit for these individuals; whereas it is an emergency measure for most of us, mustered when the going gets rough and the odds are against us.

Do you remember the Apollo XIII moonshot, when an essential part of the power system of the command module blew out during lunar orbit. Through a happy combination of control center ingenuity, superb spacemanship, and a generous dose of divine providence, the ship was able to limp safely back to earth by linking with the power source of the LEM, the lunar landing vehicle. Once debriefed, the crew of Apollo XIII was swarmed upon by press people, one of whom put this question to Jack Swigert, the non-chalant bachelor among the three astronauts: "When you were out there in space, and there was serious question whether your craft could be reprogrammed for successful return to earth, did you find yourself, perhaps, uttering some sort of aspiration to some unseen force in the universe?" Swigert, at first puzzled by the wording, broke into a smile and replied, "If you are asking whether I prayed to God that we would get home safely, you bet your life I did!" Crisis can be the catalyst that moves us to pray. O'Neill's character John Loving experiences the needed restorative of divine love when he is brought to his knees in prayer because of the imminent death of his wife.

The act of prayer carries with it an implicit affirmation of faith in the presence of the divine. When you or anyone sincerely prays, you know that you are not talking to yourself. You are not "out of your tree," as they say. In your prayer you truly believe that someone is listening to you and that this someone cares for you. Even railing against God for letting evil happen to you implies a belief in the goodness of God. For if God were a malevolent being, then evil could only be expected. So when Dostoevsky avows that "if the world allows the torture of an innocent child by a brute, I hand in my ticket,"[7] he is not blaming God for man's mysterious potential for depravity. The price of being human is the suffering imposed by other humans—as the nail wounds in Jesus' body testify. Though in his final agony he would gasp forth the verse of Psalm 22, "My God, my God, why hast Thou forsaken me," Jesus expires with the essence of every prayer upon his lips, "Father, into Thy hands I commit my spirit" (Lk 23:46).

Prayer is at once healing and vocational, because in dissolving our fears with divine love it also revitalizes our unique spirit. This is the aspect of prayer that W.H. Auden describes:

> If I talk about prayer, I think the petitionary side of it is purely a preliminary, superficial thing, because it is quite involuntary. Naturally, we are always asking: Can I marry the girl I love? Can I sell my house? or whatever. But a prayer really begins at the point at which one listens to a voice. I am not going to argue with people about this; I would call it the voice of the Holy Spirit, you could call it the inner light. The only things you cannot call it, you cannot call it reason, and you cannot call it the superego because the superego could never say anything new.[8]

Auden's description of prayer reminds me of one of my last conversations with John Macmurray, who in his gentle kindness showed the sincere regard for others that was the very lifeblood of his teaching and writing. I had asked him quite plainly why he believed in God. His answer sparkled in its lucid simplicity: "Because of our pressure to communicate, there must be a responsive being there to listen."

This presence of a listening God is what evoked from Saint-Exupéry the prayer on the final pages of *Citadelle*, his magnum opus, that was published posthumously: "O Lord, in You alone, love and friendship are truly knit and it is Your will that I shall not reach them except in your silence."[9] This mirrors St-Ex's conviction that "love is first of all the exercise of prayer and prayer the exercise of silence."[10] Prayer for Saint-Exupéry gives us access to the God of Love, who clears the self-centered fear from the wellsprings of our uniqueness, releasing the spontaneous flow of total gift that instills friendship.

The silence of prayer hollows out a harbor of quiet from the pressures and preoccupations that claim our attention. Prayer is the respite that allows us to return to the still center of our uniqueness where the deep currents of our unnamed aspirations are pulsing, where an almost palpable movement from the originating source of our being stirs us forth from the protective cover that inhibits us. Our hearts are drying up. We are thirsty for the waters Jesus spoke about to the Samaritan woman that day at the well of Jacob. Prayer is the channel to this restorative; and the Gospel can provide specific focus for our yearning.

The conversation, for instance, that John reports between Jesus and the outcast Samaritan woman carries encouragement for every one of us. Jesus offers the "living water" of belonging to a woman who was then living with a man after her five marriages had broken up. She is desperate for the touch of divine love that will revive her parched spirit. One sentence from Jesus does it—"I who speak with you am he" (Jn 4:26), the one who has the words of eternal life. In her joy at being able to lead her own life again, free from the taints and taunts that had made her come to the well alone, the woman seeks out the townfolk to announce, "Come and see a man who has told me everything I ever did" (John 4: 29). Jesus knows all about her, though he had never set eyes on her before. Could he not be reaching her as the divine source of her personal uniqueness, in keeping with his veiled identity that is the leitmotiv of John's gospel?

If this be so, Jesus' sympathetic words reach beyond the unnamed woman of Sychar and come to rest on each of us because they are spoken by the one who is as much the source of our unique spirit as hers. The tender concern that Jesus shows for this disillusioned lady or for Peter or Magdalene carries over to us because we are also the Father's beloved for whom his divine Son became incarnate. Our prayer is bolstered by these accents of love that leap from the Gospel text. The brilliant light that shines from Jesus' noonday dialogue with the woman at the well arches the centuries. How rare an instance in human history for an ordinary person like you or me to be having a

100

heart-to-heart talk with the one person who knows all about us because he is the creative source of our personal spirit, the one who assured his opponents that "Before Abraham came to be, I am" (Jn 8:58). This is why we cling to the Gospel words; we sense that they are also addressed to us. Prayerful reflection upon the human phrases of the Divine Son serve as our reservoir of refreshment as we plumb the depths where the springs of divine love still flow in the personal universe.

It is striking that in his parable Saint-Exupéry finally came to know the little prince at a well in the desert in a starlit interlude that reminded the aviator of Christmas Eve and midnight Mass. We too are pulled from our lonely fears with the reassurance in belonging that divine love instills in us. Our prayerful conversation leads us beyond scriptural meditation in our chosen nook to liturgical celebration of Christmas, Good Friday, and Easter. The shared prayer of these communal rites also kindles within us the warmth of divine love, thawing the most intransigent roots of isolation. The worshiping community, for John Macmurray, offers the main access to the divine presence:

> For the Christian, in his worship of God, there is, however, another experience, that of the presence of Jesus Christ in and amongst the worshippers. And this presence seems, as it were to coalesce with, or join itself to the presence of God, in such fashion as to provide the image of God that we need.[11]

Macmurray has cut to the heart of the Incarnational mystery. Yet the pivotal point still presses: how do we actually encounter God and his saving graciousness amongst our fellow humans? The simple though ultimately unfathomable response to this fundamental question harks back to the Gospels and, especially, to the First Letter of John that declares: "Though God has never been seen by any man, God himself dwells in us if we love one another; his love is brought to perfection within us" (1 Jn 4:12).

My experience of the spontaneous, self-forgetting love that another person shows to me is the hint of God's love coming my way, if I only have the awareness to recognize it. Certainly I can find no reason within myself for this person's selfless generosity toward me. Why should he turn away from his own pursuits and legitimate self-interest to attend to my needs? When the ill-fated Air Florida jet plunged into the Potomac River one wintry day in 1982, what inspired passerby Lenny Skutnik to dive into the icy waters to rescue a woman passenger who had lost her grip on the lifeline? Instinct? Hardly, since others on the shore did not budge. There must have been another dynamic at work. What is it that impels a person like Lenny Skutnik to set aside his own self-interest and risk his life for an unknown stranger? Theologian Karl Rahner would reply, reinforcing John Macmurray's view, that this is an instance of the divine spirit of love coursing through that person's uniqueness, lifting him across the threshold of sacrifice for his neighbor.

For Rahner, the neighbor—whether stranger or close friend—becomes the providential "angel" releasing that surge of total love wherein we experience God in our unreserved sharing: "We can say that the person who is the object of our love is the real mediator in our relationship to God, that through him or her we achieve direct contact with God."[12]

Seen from this vantage point, selfless human love is actually the thrust of divine love making itself felt in our interpersonal relationships. Père Duval, the French singer whom Rahner admired, puts this momentous truth into the lyrics of his song, *"Au Coin de Ma Rue."* The guitar-priest says that God is not to be found beyond the clouds nor at the end of the world; no, He is at the corner of my street! To dramatize the presence of the divine Son among us, Père Duval sings of the engaged couple:

> When you spoke kind things to me, my dear,
> He wasn't far from us—
> When you spoke kind things to me,
> It was his tenderness that was already singing forth!

In this perspective there is only one love in the personal universe, the love of the divine Son for the Father. And we are called to participate in that love because we are linked to that Son's humanity. This Incarnational love becomes the human response to the Father's boundless love for his Son, a love that embraces us also. Consequently, every sincere gesture of other-centered love that we offer to one another is a sharing in the divine Son's dedication to his Father and is enkindled by their mutual Spirit of divine love.

When your dearest friend remembers your birthday with a present, he is saying, "I love you always." Yet there is a deeper significance that goes beyond the article beneath the wrappings. In the gift your friend is also saying that you are so dear that if the occasion arose he would give everything, even life itself, for you. This is the Incarnational view of total commitment. It was this same interpersonal dedication that led countless soldiers, sailors, airmen, and civilians to give their lives during World War II. The banner beneath which they fell was their country's; the beloved, however, was the wife, the child, the parent, the fiancee whose wrinkled photo was next their heart when they died. Saint-Exupéry spoke for all in writing to his friend, "If I go back to battle, it will be . . . for the return of your smile."[13] These personal sacrifices were the supreme realization of Jesus' words: "Greater love than this no man has, that a man should lay down his life for his friends" (Jn 15:13). Total self-giving is the glow of divine love in our midst.

Prayer raises our consciousness of God's presence in our world, while the Gospel accounts of Jesus' words and deeds fix our interior focus. Vibrant liturgical celebrations enliven our sense of belonging to one another in the bond of community instilled by Jesus. But with this Incarnational perspective brought to light through prayer and worship, it is the welcoming love of my friend that ultimately breaks through the clouds of doubt and mistrust and enfolds me with a sense of the presence of God surrounding me. It is the constant care of Christmas, the unconditional forgiveness of Calvary, and the unwavering hope of Easter. This perfect Incarnational love, the radical solution for self-protective fear, is able to transform my characteristic disposition into an other-centered attitude.

# SIX

## *The Character of Love*

The centerpiece of Jesus' religious movement is love, love as a pervasive, emotional disposition tilted in favor of the neighbor rather than back upon self. Love blossoms into other meanings: the affection for your beloved, the action of charity that is "care for You," and the bond of belonging that mutual affection creates, and the reciprocal dedication of genuine care strengthens. But neither the action of love nor the union of love can arise except from a heart whose prevailing dispostion is other-centered. This is the positive characteristic in a person that Saint Paul extols in his classic hymn to love:

> Love is patient; love is kind and envies no one. Love is never boastful, nor conceited, nor rude; never selfish, not quick to take offence. Love keeps no score of wrongs; does not gloat over other men's sins, but delights in the truth. There is nothing love cannot face; there is no limit to its faith, its hope, and its endurance (1 Cor 13:4–7).

When Jesus preached a "change of heart," he was cutting away at the self-centered tangle of fear which snarls every human being. Overweaning fear makes a person insincere! As persons we are called to resplendent dedication to another, yet we while away our days in dull, defensive self-interest, under the various guises it can assume. The hollowest form of such self-centeredness is putting on the facade of love.

Beguiling charm passes itself off as tender affection. Possessive delight in or demand for the friend's companionship masquerades as dedication. Sexual desire engages a pliant partner with the counterfeit avowal of undying devotion. "Soap-opera" catchwords ensnare the heart of another while the focus of interest has never shifted from self. Treasuring his "lady-love" for the pleasure of her company or exploiting her for sexual passion, for all its candlelight romance, never says more than "you are a value to me for *my* sake." This is suave insincerity compared to the bona fide love that declares with full heart, "You are a value to me for *your* sake!" You are the center of interest.

The curse of the Playboy mentality that has infected a large segment of American society for a quarter century is that it has fostered this charade as part of its macho image of masculinity and, more deplorably, has duped too many women into believing that they cannot hope for better. This fraudulent tampering with the ways of intimate personal relationship is, in the mind of John Macmurray, fraught with devastating implications:

> This identification of love with sex, which is now so widespread, and which has received scientific sanctification in the psychology of the Freudian school, is merely an instance of the error which identifies the personal with the organic...But it is the most disastrous because the most intimate and effective instance. It is not too much to say, perhaps, that unless this form of our most radical error is overcome, it must destroy our civilization. [1]

Self-interest, however reciprocal, when it intrudes upon the most delicate symbolism of total dedication eventually brings utter disillusionment and a depressed sense of self-worth. In John Macmurray's estimate it is this underlying insincerity that makes the particular liaison unchaste:

> But sexual desire is not love. Desire is quite compatible with personal hatred, or contempt, or indifference, because it treats its object not as a person but as a means to its own satisfaction... Mutual desire does not make things any better. It only means that each of two persons is treating the other as a means of self-satisfaction... It is the desire to obtain possession of another person for the satisfaction of their own needs; to dare to assert the claim over another human being—"You are mine!" That is unchaste and immoral, a definite inroad upon the integrity of a fellow human being... Mutual love is the only basis of a human relationship; and bargains and claims and promises are attempts to substitute something else; and they introduce falsity and unchastity into the relationship.[2]

The time-hallowed symbolism of sexual union is total dedication. To engage in this specific expression of intimacy without the grounding of mutual love is to bar oneself from authentic closeness in personal relationship. Sexual union without the implicit commitment of genuine love blocks the approaches to interior personal communication and trust and reduces this human interaction to a mere surface association. Sexuality without the dedication of friendship is superficial because such physical snugness is empty of personal meaning. The reality and significance of personal union become more illusive in the scruffy nest of reciprocal self-gratification, an inevitable diminishing that John Macmurray accurately diagnoses:

> When people enjoy themselves through each other, that is merely mutual lust. They do not meet as persons at all; their reality is lost. They meet as ghosts of themselves and their pleasure is a ghostly pleasure that cannot begin to satisfy a human soul, and which vitiates its capacity for reality.[3]

This imposter for the graciousness of other-centered devotion delivers sensate pleasure but not the peace of belonging. This is why Saint-Exupéry considers the feverishness of irresistible desire to be spurious as love:

> Do not confuse love with the rapture of possession which brings the cruelest of suffering. For, contrary to the popular notion, love does not foment suffering. What causes suffering is possessive desire which is the opposite of love.... True love begins where nothing is looked for in return.[4]

Saint-Exupéry and John Macmurray complement one another in their refrain that love is, in essence, other-centered, and that sexual desire can undermine this sense of devotedness, if sought for its own sake. Macmurray goes so far as to say that sexual expression must await the union of friendship already formed and firmly implanted before it can be a sincere gesture of that friendship. For him an authentic bond of belonging involves "an emotional unity between a man and a woman which transcends egoism and selfish desire." He expands his meaning:

> In such a unity sex ceases to be an appetite—a want to be satisfied—and becomes a means of communion, simple and natural. Mutual self-satisfaction is incompatible with chastity, which demands the expression of a personal unity already secured... Sex-love, if it is love at all, is a personal communion in which a man and a woman meet in the full integrity of their personal reality.[5]

What a contrast the personal vision of Macmurray and Saint-Exupéry is to the presentations of contemporary media productions that would entice our teenagers into thinking that sexual intimacy is the avenue to friendship. To the astounding credit of our good, good young people and their families, they refuse, in steady self-assurance, to stoop to the demeaning profiles by which a certain coterie of television and movie directors are inclined to portray them. Our youth remain strong in honoring a noble, worthy image of themselves, marvelously unsullied by the truck purveyed by some media entrepreneurs. They are wise enough to know, even in their early years, that, as Saint-Exupéry puts it, "the value of a gift depends upon who receives it."[6] The gift of love is drained of personal worth when the one to whom it is directed is preoccupied with selfish desire. With such a person, "you would not have begun to *give*. For there is no one to receive."[7] When sexual gratification is paramount for the one, its preemption is hardly the acceptance of gift, however much the other may intend it to be so. The other-centered quality of authentic love as a characteristic disposition cannot abide the inroads of self-interest of any kind, particularly in the mutuality of sexual intimacy.

Such exploitation of another is a form of intensive control over another, which is a symptom of self-protective fear. For all its popularity, this behavior treats the other as "threat" to one's realization as a person. He is afraid to wait upon the promptings of her heart and the glad spontaneity of her devotion. Consequently, this commandeered attention through his sexual demand (or her obvious availability) reveals a clutching fear of isolation that cannot trust that the other will love him for himself. He chooses to ignore the maxim that love can neither be forced nor organized.

Possessiveness and jealousy in a relationship are other manifestations of this same sort of defensive self-interest. This is why John Macmurray drops the subtle remark that there can be no true *amour a deux*:

> Any real fellowship achieved between persons spills over, as it were, into the desire to share it. It cannot do otherwise. When any fellowship becomes exclusive, it ceases to be a real fellowship and becomes a mere defensive alliance to safeguard common interests.[8]

Other-centered love is universal to its core because in barring even one person as a threat to our relationship we render ourselves vulnerable to the inroads of self-protective fear which could eventually taint the bond with our beloved. What you love in your friend is precisely her unique spirit, her special way of making gift. So when she opens her heart to others and they in turn claim her time because of their urgent distress, this in no way diminishes her regard for you. You are the still-center for all her giving to others because you are her identifying friend. You are not neglected, nor is your relationship jeopardized by her devotedness to your children or to the needy neighbor down the street. You are unusually blessed that such a great-hearted person, so cherished in your tiny section of the globe, should have chosen you to become the focus of her own history here.

Your friend's open-hearted attitude actually intensifies her love for you in your unwillingness to put any strictures upon her spontaneity through some kind of misguided tactic to limit intrusions upon your time and household. There is a rhythm in all of these moments tumbling upon one another that her primary devotion to you settles upon. There is a time for company and a time to be alone; a time to celebrate your belonging with your friend and a time when you are both inclined to seek out the silence of prayer to your God.

The universality inherent in this other-centered disposition of love is, in John Macmurray's view, an axiom for personal fulfillment: "The self-realization of any individual is only fully achieved if he is positively motived towards every other person with whom he is in relation."[9] The heart of charity is incompatible with an unresolved fear that could corrode the benign, serenely open attitude toward others. Other-centered love extends to all those people we already know and to those we may yet come to know. Its opposite number is the pervasive fear that is also all-encompassing and mistrusts long-standing companions as well as unknown strangers. It shows its head as prejudice against the "enemy" one has never met. This is why Jesus stressed a totally comprehensive charity with his injunction, "Love your enemies." Such charity implies the forgiving attitude that Jesus set up as the keystone of personal relationships.

This not only allows other-centered love to reach the unique reality of the individual member of a maligned group whom I am about to encounter. This forgiving ingredient in the open disposition of other-centered love applies particularly to the friend I know well who may have slighted my devotedness, thereby igniting the coals of unlikely hatred in my heart. Unlike the dominant fear that spreads indiscriminately to old acquaintances and anonymous bystanders, hatred is specific. British psychologist Ian Suttie has concluded that "hatred, except for a preferred rival or a rejecting lover does not seem to exist."[10] It is visited upon that particular person in whom you have placed your hopes and commitment for your personal realization. In her rejection of you, the sources of your aspirations and happiness dry up and, in Macmurray's analysis, she comes to "threaten your existence as a person in an absolute fashion."[11]

Hatred is triggered by the possible loss of a significant relationship. It fixes upon the person who was once the very life of me. John Macmurray's definition is right on the mark: "Hatred is love frustrated by fear."[12] This is why Othello's striking at Desdemona is not really a death-wish but the dire demand for her love, which, in the wild imaginings fueled by Iago, she has removed from him in favor of Cassio. Othello's assault is against the removal of Desdemona's love, though in the agonized sweep of his lethal arm, he dooms his beloved along with himself. His hatred is a double annihilation—the source of his personal realization, Desdemona, and himself.

Because personal realization depends upon the loving response of the "You," and because, as Macmurray points out, "it is impossible that you should always be able to respond to me in the way that my action expects,"[13] the seeds of hatred are present in every relationship. This is why forgiveness is such an essential strand in the basic weave of other-centered love between spouses and closest friends. Giving your friend the benefit of the doubt through your kind regard for her is the best way of curbing jealousy, self-pity, and envy—those petty resentments that carry the seed of hatred.

The most difficult test, however, for the strength of one's spirit of forgiveness comes when a relationship actually breaks down and you experience the overwhelming, unaccountable disdain of the girl you had called your bride and the mother of your children. Abandoned and bruised at heart, you still have the responsibility for her and for the children entrusted to your care. It would be easy and quite understandable for you to turn bitter at this set-back in your personal life that has brought so much anguish. Your character of other-centered love is sorely tried and you are strongly tempted to engage in good old-fashioned retaliation, as if there were such an acceptable mockery of what Jesus stood for. You would like to "shake the dust from your feet," the biblical gesture of disengagement from those who have refused the greeting of "peace to this house." But you don't have it in you to do this. Why? Because you are keeping true to your other-centered character and to its Christian response of forgiveness in the face of the rupture of a bond to which you had given everything—time, energy, livelihood, and love. To turn bitter would be to compound the trouble by poisoning the positive outlook that had been the distinguishing mark of your personal makeup.

By comparison with this assault upon your happiness, the Nazi atrocities cry to heaven for vengeance. But even here, heaven should be the ultimate arbiter rather than that relentless pressing for redress should embitter the hearts of the Nazi-hunters. Deny forgiveness, and both hunted and hunter wither as humans. The weightier matters of the Law, in Jesus' revision, were justice, mercy, and trustworthiness.[14] Without the healing of forgiveness to mellow our human relationships, the nobility and grace and peace of belonging in home and in friendship are ever beyond reach.

The merciful heart of a person who can withstand the hurt of a devastating split in the fabric of close relationship must have mined a deeper vein of personal union that was not crushed by the abrupt walk-out of the one who had meant most. This had already been accomplished in prayer. His habitual recourse to God had given him this sense of belonging to the "Father" which preserved him from any absolute peril to his own realization. The same divine love that is the radical solution to his anxiety about possible isolation had instilled a tranquillity in his heart that is proof against all turbulence.

He has known the peace of being son of the Father. He is always "at home," so that his sense of belonging does not rise or fall with the mood swings in the behavior of his friends or his spouse's full-scale barrage upon the structure of his living.

In his prayer he has experienced the meaning of Paul's line in the Epistle to the Romans, "His [God's] Spirit [of love] assures our spirit that we are the children of God" (Rm 8:16). Oh, he is no saint. He is subject to emotional undertows and, too often, caves in to selfishness and to angry outbursts. But prayer has given him a listening heart that knows the peace of belonging always to the Father in Christ, and so he is ready to forgive his errant wife or recalcitrant child because each is forever the specially beloved child of God, our Father.

He will not let wounded pride shut the door on the hope of reconciliation with the friend or spouse who has dealt him such heavy havoc. His prayer has prevented any traces of resentment from hardening his heart. He can forgive because his personal fulfillment, in an ultimate way, was never in danger. Consequently he will not be party to that unfortunate impasse of the estranged couple Macmurray describes:

> Each of them feels wronged by the other. The natural tendency of each in reflection is, therefore, to accuse the other, to fix the blame for the break upon the other, and so to increase his own isolation and to thwart tendencies to reconciliation. In that state of alienation, reconciliation is impossible. [15]

His own willingness to forgive rules out the stance that would close off all avenues to repentance and reconciliation.

Prayer has woven into his interior spirit a tightly knit bond to God that not only prompts his merciful gesture toward a disloyal friend but has also created such a sense of personal fulfillment at the core of his being that he is now completely free for gift to others. Because the meaning of his personal existence has a firm basis in his tie with God as his "constant You," he will not be inclined to manipulate a friend to shore up those gaps of isolation that all of us are subject to. "'Tis the blight that man is born for, 'tis Margaret that you mourn for"[16] is Gerard Manley Hopkins's way of describing our long loneliness with its attendant fears that is the ultimate, residual sign of human-kind's primordial cleavage from God. But no human person can fill up that void in my yearning for relationship, because no other than God as the source of my personal spirit can totally know me in my uniqueness and therefore love me just as I am in my unvarnished reality. Consequently, any attempt of mine to latch onto another human, even a closest friend, to ward off the weary desperation of loneliness would be neither love nor gift to that other.

This is why it is so important that no one marry who cannot live by himself or herself as a mature adult. In coming to terms with the ever-present mystery of human loneliness—the price of our individuality—we can trace to the very depths of our being that unique longing for realization that rides upon our every heartbeat. There, at the core of our identity, we can come to realize through prayer that our uniqueness has no final significance other than that we be the beloved of the Father as the creative source of our personal spirit.

In the radiance of that ennobling light, we can appreciate all the more the part that our parents, friends, and family have played in calling forth our own uniqueness. In not expecting them to understand all that we are longing to become, we can sympathize with their being puzzled at our traveling a road in life that they really cannot fathom, nor perhaps even approve. But because we are imbued with a sense of belonging to the God who does countenance our every "push" toward self-transcendence, we will not impose ourselves upon others nor force them to implement our plans. Quite the other way around. Our ventures are attuned to their needs because in a fundamental way our life is already complete because we have found belonging through the Incarnational perspective of prayer. We as mature adults are now ready for the total gift of self in friendship or for the identifying relationship that is marriage. The distinguishing character of other-centered love has become so well-rounded and integral in us that we are poised for the committed action of love that, in its loyal dedication, builds personal union—the one achievement that can fill a person's life and satisfy the heart.

# SEVEN

## *Love in Action*

The other-centered person trusts the invitation to friendship. He is keenly aware of the person near him, respects her uniqueness, and waits upon her hint of response to his interest—"What is essential is invisible to the eye; it is only with the heart that one can see rightly." In the rapport he has found with the innermost sources of his personal spirit, that font that Jesus had said would spring up to eternal life, his search for fulfilling friendship can abide the time for total gift. Should she choose to say Yes, without even pronouncing that single syllable, yet resoundingly announce it with her welcoming smile, then the currents of their separate histories would flow together. The first tendernesses of friendship would have been exchanged; no—the invitations would have been exchanged, but the respective initiatives toward the other would be sifted into that vibrant commingling that is relationship.

The blend of the bond "takes" because of the unique "gift" that each friend brings. The relationship is enriched by the very

115

differences that go to make up each person. Their mutual choice
to share their lives in the complete equality of friendship opens
the mystery of each in the fulness of trusting communication.
Their mutual gift of themselves to one another melds the
relationship, allowing each to experience the warm glow of the
other's interest and affection.

This is the paradox that John Macmurray describes: "The
difference between 'I' and 'you' is of the very essence of
personality. There is no 'I' without a 'you.' The relationship
between persons constitutes their individual personality."[1] The
sparkling grandeur of the shared relationship itself is what is
vital to each friend. It is not a drab partnership serving
reciprocal self-interest that either could shelve at the drop of a
hat. No, this is their own unique union in personal belonging,
drawing forth the full capacity for dedication in each one. This is
the ultimate personal value that engages the full energy,
enthusiasm, and elation of responsible choice at the unique
center of each person. Touched with the grace of healing love
that has dispersed the last traces of self-protective fear, each
friend rejoices in the revelation of the loving "You" that unveils
the glorious vista of belonging which imparts lasting significance to human life. For a bride and her groom this mutual
choice is expressed in the "I do" of their wedding day. They join
in a commitment to action, the action of mutual charity which
alone sustains, enriches, and strengthens sincere friendship.

## Morality as Consistent Action

We have entered the realm of morality, properly speaking.
For morality is consistent action leading to a chosen value.
Without a morality our lives would have neither shape nor
direction. The career of our days would then simply be random
careening from episode to episode and falling out at the finish,
no matter what gains came our way. This kind of vulnerability
to the crosscurrents of our personal histories is not "us," as we
say, because our prerogative of freedom is not engaged. No, as
persons we are called upon to take charge and participate in the
helmsmanship that will guide us to the harbor of our deepest
longings. Consequently, we do sail "to the stars" and adhere to

some sort of charting as we each steer a steady course to whatever achievement we have set our heart upon. We act as moral persons in embracing a goal and following it through to the finish.

There was a time when we thought that human morality was observing a set of rules. Such obedience, however, is not our own personal morality because the norms were not of our own choosing. They were imposed by authority. Of course, obedience to guidelines laid down by parents, school, or church is a proper avenue of growth for the young child. By insisting on good manners and our "picking up" our room, our parents shaped within us a way of looking after our deportment and getting along with others that serves us well in later life. These habits have freed us for the important matters in human interchange. Our parents also taught us the difference between right and wrong. But as mature adults we must appropriate whatever standards we actually decide to live by as part of our own responsible choice; otherwise these are not so much a matter of our morality as of our acquiescence.

The tragic abdication of morality in the name of obedience to *der Fuhrer* by so many Nazi judges, guards, and storm troopers is one of the tawdriest chapters in modern history. These people had accepted the premise that somehow obedience exempted a person from responsibility for his or her own actions. The terror of the Gestapo, of course, was pressing these men and women to betray their humanity. Ironically, it was their victims, like Jean Moulin of the French underground, who rescued human dignity by surmounting even the fear of death to reconstitute the moral fiber of a devastated Europe.

The responsibility to direct my life through my own mature decision and action is, in the final accounting, nontransferable. Adam would blame Eve for enticing him to the forbidden fruit, but the divine keeper of Eden was not impressed with his defense. Each of us by our own doing inscribes our own particular history. Certain chapters we would, in retrospect, revise. But all we can do is make amends, since past deeds are indelibly written into our biography. The sticking-point of morality is that it implies an identification with the value I adopt with the total measure of my freedom. The choice is mine. Since I have embraced a particular value or goal as my own, I also accept the specific line of action that will bring that objective to fruition.

There are a variety of "moralities" prevalent in our world, as any glance at the newspaper will remind us. In this mixture of codes of conduct, there is often obvious conflict. The gentle largesse of an Italian pope like John XXIII was a far cry from the "gutter" morals of the Red Brigade or the Mafia underworld. Closer to home, our hybrid culture in the United States attempts to walk the tightrope between the norms of those citizens who favor abortion as a woman's "right" and those who consider it to be a lethal assault upon an innocent human who deserves the protection of the law. How long any country can survive without an internally consistent ethical stance is the hidden issue here. This particular attempt to implement a pluralistic morality, through the blessing of the Supreme Court, would bestow the seal of approval upon contradictory moral practices. The thorny question whether or not such an amalgam can work in some sort of framework of "peaceful coexistence" puts public morality on tenterhooks, jeopardizing any cohesive sense of a national ethic for the citizens of the United States.

## Care for You

However, the cycles of legal, political, and social morality aside, at the *personal* level of existence there can be only one ultimate principle of morality for each of us, and that is charity. The compelling reason is elemental: Since personal realization comes about only in the full mutuality of personal belonging, there is but one consistent action that can accomplish this, namely, the charity that is "care for you." All other lines of deliberate action, whether in organization, business, cooperative enterprise, or leisure-time pursuits are, in themselves, "care for self," however legitimate and praiseworthy these various endeavors may be. We are caught up in these individual ventures each time we go off to work on Monday or to sailing on a Sunday. Not that these particular activities are necessarily *individualistic*! The person we say good-bye to in the morning and whose smile greets us upon our return in the evening is the one we care for, the one for whom we set out to work in the first place.

Yet in stepping off the bus or clambering from the commuter train into the swirl of the marketplace, we are immersed in a competitive whirlpool. An easy surmise, therefore, would be that on the weekend we would seek respite from this incessant struggle to gain the advantage that is the lifestream of the business world. Mercifully, many of us can and do draw the curtain on the ups and downs that mark our week on the job when we cross the threshold of home on the weekend.

There are others, however, in whom the inner clock of competition refuses to wind down. So on Saturday, the "go-getter" of industry wields a different weapon, this time a racquet, as he battles for the gold medal in the club tennis tournament. He is in step with our culture that has cast an aura of admiration around winning in sports. The awarding of the trophy, for instance, in the Master's Golf Tournament before the national television audience has all the trappings of ecclesiastical ritual. The "elders," jacketed in their vestments of green with the coveted insignia on the breast pocket, escort the victor into the inner circle and clothe him with his own dalmatic of knighthood in golf.

This near-solemn ceremonial of competitive success spotlights the peak of achievement in a particular frame of living. The crucial question underlying all this display, however, is what place this honor holds in the hierarchy of a person's values. Has this golf or tennis championship been won, perhaps, at the neglect of the awkward, non-athletic eleven-year-old son back at the house who whiles away his time glued to the television set, manipulating an Atari game because his dad's too busy to go hiking.

In the same vein, another story may be unfolding beneath the slightly drawn expression of the corporate manager who guides his eldest daughter up the aisle on her wedding day. His somber countenance could mask an inner regret that his desire to garner individual laurels even on his weekends had deprived

119

him of the company of this beautiful twenty-two-year-old woman whom he now knows too little and who today is leaving his home for good. Concern for his own success at work and at play had cramped his time with, if not his devotion for this daughter. As he slowly passes the faces of the guests in church, a flood of images scoot by the screen of his memory in slide-show fashion: of a little bundle of curls in a swing at the park, the kindergartener in her polished black shoes, the child-madonna on her First Communion day, the gangling eighth-grader with braces on her teeth and her arm in a sling after a fall from her bike, the sixteen-year-old going to her first high school prom, and the white-gowned graduate, first from the local high school and, just recently, the college where she met this fine, likeable boy whose family name she will presently assume. He realizes in a flash that he really hadn't been at home for her that much during her last ten years with him and Mom.

Oh, the wedding announcement in tomorrow's *Times* will mention that he is currently a senior vice-president. How very *senior* he feels—old, that is—in giving away his beloved daughter. As he approaches the transept where the sprightly, nervous groom awaits his handshake, something recoils inside. An interior voice urges, "Wait! I don't want to ever give you away; you are the very life of me." Almost imperceptibly he falters; but what must be, must be—and his daughter's happiness must *be*! As he lifts the veil to kiss her good-bye, God be with you always, her gentle radiance touched with the tear-trace at the edge of her eyes pushes the words to his lips that he now wishes he somehow had spoken each evening, "Thank you, angel, for your stay with us."

She has been an angel of forgiveness to him, overlooking his inability too often to shift mental gears when he got home from work, forgetting that his family was not his firm, that he was not competing with his two sons and two daughters or his wife, that efficient productivity was not the hallmark of home, that the unique worth of each member had nothing to do with prizes or bonuses.

As she turns from him to go up to the altar of God to consecrate her love to her husband, this firstborn child also becomes an angel of revelation for him. She has called him back to himself. The trophies lining the top shelf in his den are tinsel to him now, compared to the time he missed with the resplendent figure before him, the daughter whose soft voice is at this very instant speaking her wedding vows. She has pulled him from the brink of the self-centered individualism that would undermine the two values that mean the most to him in life, family and friendship. The other three children and his wife will be the beneficiaries of the inner conversion that this lovely person leaving his home has wrought in him. Never again will he let self-preoccupied pursuits steer him away from his primary concern for the particular "you"'s in his life. This, the first wedding within his family, has put his whole adult history into review, like a shaft of sunlight breaking through the overcast of weekly routine.

In this moment of illumination he has detected the pitfall that awaits the person who lets individual self-interest at work or at play turn into *individualistic* self-centeredness. The cumulative effect on the person whose predominant morality is care for self at the expense of others is the utter individualism that is total isolation. The man who has no room in his heart for others during his relentless drive to the apex of individual power, wealth, fame, or achievement will find there is no room for others at the top either. The point of the pyramid he piled up through disregard and exploitation of others is the pinnacle of loneliness.

Rugged individualism carries within itself the seeds of its own destruction: all-consuming care for self turns away the sincere friends who might discern the person behind the ribbons of renown. These are mere glitter devoid of meaning without the warming regard of friends who would have continued to esteem the man for himself, with or without the medals.

Epic figures like Abraham Lincoln and Charles de Gaulle lived by the wisdom that reserved a special place in their hearts for family and good friends. The astute tactics, brilliant strategies, and hard-nosed decisions each was called upon to take in his critical hour on the ramparts of human history never compromised the care for others that was his bedrock, integrating morality. Lincoln had to ride head-on into the maelstrom of the slavery question that would tear the nation in two. But during those darkest hours of the Civil War, Lincoln looked forward to the evening hour when he could read to his son Tad.

Nearly a century later Charles de Gaulle, after a draining day in his Champs Élysées chambers hammering out a new constitution for post-war France, would walk the tree-lined garden at dusk, hand-in-hand with his daughter Anne. The towering figure of the French general, bending over to catch the dancing impressions of his beloved child, together with the care-worn countenance of Lincoln, interpreting a story with full gusto for his rambunctious eight-year-old, present indelible images of home, belonging, and of the *whole* person who has anchored his morality in charity. Neither de Gaulle nor Lincoln entertained the least notion that they were doing their children a favor—it never crossed their minds. Quite the other way around! Both leaders treasured the equilibrium in living that the company of their children restored in them.

Perhaps the reason why these leaders were such formidable protagonists in the years of their nations' grimmest crises was that they had long since set their priorities straight, with neither one relishing a round of battle for its own sake. It took a de Gaulle to kneel in Rheims cathedral with Konrad Adenauer, the Chancellor of Germany, France's ancient enemy, to seal a compact of reconciliation and peace. Similarly, Lincoln's last message before he was shot to death was one of overriding zeal to heal the wounds of the defeated Confederacy. These were men of true wisdom whose biographies bear out the sweeping axiom of John Macmurray: "All meaningful knowledge is for the sake of action and all meaningful action, for the sake of friendship."[2]

The integrating action of love transfigures all the hours we spend in contract negotiations at work or scrapping for the decisive point in recreational tennis into channels of devotion for family or friend. The needed restorative of a morning of golf can return a refreshened husband and father to the kitchen to help his wife wash down the walls or help his teenage daughter with a math problem. This man next door could be Abe Lincoln reading to Tad or Charles de Gaulle walking along in conversation with Anne.

In the end it all comes back to conversation! For conversation is of the essence of home, belonging, and friendship—conversation in its basic sense of being "turned toward you" in interest and dedication. The bride and groom on their wedding day *turn toward* one another to exchange their vows and slip the rings on each other's finger as a sign of their oneness.

In a real sense friendship is always a "conversation" between the "You" and the "I," even though no words are spoken, strolling along together at the beach in summer, in the woods at autumn, and towards home throughout life. Friendship allows for pauses; the silence intimates no lack of communication because each has given himself or herself away to the other. Talk is not necessarily revelation of oneself, as any sampling of Johnny Carson's "Tonight Show" will verify. A barrage of chitchat can turn meaning off. The quiet conversation of friends is the essence of communication and the heart of belonging. In this warming glow, the dreary discouragement of setbacks at the office fades away while a new bounce comes back to one's step. The heartening brightness in the eyes of my friend reflects her delight in the small accomplishment that I have finally managed after months of late night effort and early morning appointments.

My friend's unwavering interest lends significance to all I do. This is why for each of us, as for bride and groom, the "care for you" that forms friendship also imparts fresh meaning to all of our individual activities. They are caught up into the orbit of friendship where we rest easy in knowing that this someone cares about what we do. This wholeness in personal living suggests a key nuance in Jesus' enigmatic statement, "If you would save your life, you will lose it. But if you lose your life, you will find it" (Lk 17:33). In losing my life in care for "you," I not only find the fulfilling value of belonging but also the enduring worth of everything else I do.

## Your Word as Friend

The specific morality of the "care for you" that shapes friendship is to keep one's word as friend. Belonging is built upon implicit trust and total sincerity. A friend is a person you can always count on "being there" for you, and you for him or her. This reminds me of an instance in the friendship of my father with his best friend Ray, one day to be my godfather. Both had taken their engineering degrees from Tufts in 1922. In the fall of '23, my father was working on a U.S. Army dam project near Harrisburg, Pennsylvania, Ray on road construction near Boston. One Thursday Ray received a one-line telegram from my father—"Meet me in New York City, Friday." As Ray recounted the tale later on, he set about looking up the Pennsylvainia R.R. runs to New York from Harrisburg, and he matched his own Boston departure to that. Upon arrival at Grand Central Station, Ray took a cab across town to Penn Station. He knew that my father would be pulling on his pipe in the depot's smoking lounge, and there Ray found him, nose buried in the *Saturday Evening Post*! My father's confidence in Ray was set in cement; he knew that, barring derailment, the two of them would celebrate a pleasant reunion that weekend in New York.

Of course today, with all our rage for progress, the complicated network of transportation and message delivery would probably have put my father on "hold," thereby hazarding the spontaneous get-together of the two friends. But the image of the two Friday afternoon trains steaming towards New York from opposite directions ages well in my memory as an excellent manifestation of trust. Friendship doesn't need an appointment ahead of time and sometimes it just cuts across encrusted routine to restate the supreme worth of this priceless bond between friends.

## Sincere Affection

Keeping one's word as friend is neither duty nor obligation for a spouse. The birthday card is not "required" nor the anniversary roses "demanded." Somehow the verse of Thomas

Moore included with the bouquet my father sent my mother on their twentieth wedding anniversary says it all:

> To keep one sacred flame
> Through life, unchilled, unmoved;
> To love in wint'ry age the same
> As first in youth we loved;
> To feel that we adore
> Even to fond excess—
> That though the heart would break with more,
> We could not live with less.[3]

The steady flame of ever-deepening friendship tries to express as best it can the heart's profound appreciation for the company, support, and dedication that our identifying friend renders to us. Moore's finely turned lines resonate with the careful measures of a Verdi opera that form the setting from which the soaring lyrics of affection arc above the "time" in one magnificent moment that casts its radiance upon everything that a friend or spouse does for the other, minute by minute, in the daily round of living.

The very sincerity of friendship urges such expression of utter gratitude to our friend for always being present to us. However, we ourselves cannot raise language to the level of the appreciation we feel for our friend. So we look to a Moore, a Saint-Exupéry, a Verdi, a Mozart to give us help. The shared experience of the beauty of *La Traviata* or *The Marriage of Figaro* is for many couples a vicarious way of expressing how precious each is to the other.

This was impressed upon me one September evening at Washington's Kennedy Center during the intermission of Massenet's *Cendrillon*. Delia Wallis as the Prince and Frederica von Stade as Cinderella had just completed their glorious love duet. And there on the outdoor veranda overlooking the Potomac with the moonlight shimmering on the water a young couple were walking arm-in-arm, obviously rejoicing in their own special belonging that the previous moment on stage had celebrated for them—as if they were the only two in all the theater. This must be why a Mozart opera composed before the inauguration of Washington, a Verdi masterpiece predating the

Civil War, and a turn-of-the-century Massenet work, all capture us completely long after other works of their age have become mere antiques. These are not period pieces. Their universal appeal lies in their open-ended symbolism in which we can enshrine our own aspirations for belonging. A Verdi becomes the voice for the dreams that we cherish with our beloved and for our appreciation of one another that we *would* communicate, if we only knew the appropriate words.

However, to suppress our inner feelings for someone out of rigid propriety or to avoid giving the impression of being "sentimental" would be a mistake. It was the uncharacteristic faltering of former Defense Secretary Robert S. McNamara in his speech christening the U.S.S. John F. Kennedy that disclosed his devotion to the late president as his dear friend. In the midst of reading his carefully prepared speech linking the mission of this aircraft carrier with the inspiration its namesake had been for him, this veteran statesman broke down in tears and could not finish. Secretary McNamara's address was the height of eloquence in its testimony of loyalty to his friend.

Sincerity in voicing the heart's meanings does sometimes overtake smooth delivery as if to underscore the pain that the loss of a friend can cause. Robert McNamara's unintentional display of affection for President Kennedy confirms what James Thurber had written in his "letter to Fred Allen in heaven," and mailed to the comedian's widow:

> Any time at all without the sound of your voice or the sight of your words on paper is bound to seem a century in length. This will, of course, be called sentimental, and it is, but there is a sincerity of friendship between men that must have a touch of sentimentality to be true.[4]

Another author, Irish playwright Brian Friel, in his bittersweet drama *Philadelphia Here I Come*, dwells upon the reluctance we all feel at times to unlock the heart's promptings that Thurber insists must be allowed to surface. A line from Walter Kerr's review of the play captures its central theme: "Not to have opened one's heart of a Sunday means to have lost a part of it by Monday, and there are now so many Mondays multiplied

126

that the very calendar of feeling has turned brown on the wall."[5]
The message is clear: Keeping your word as friend involves not
only "being there" in the resourcefulness of trust but also "to
say so" at an impromptu moment with the uncluttered spontaneity of loving regard shown in a small gift, an unobtrusive
gesture, or an off-the-cuff compliment.

## Presence

Being present is itself a sign of affection, an assurance that
you would not want to be anywhere but with your friend. This
quiet devotion was apparent in the distress of Nancy Reagan
that she had not been with her husband when he was struck by
the bullet of a would-be assassin. This was the anguish of the
great trapeze artist, Alfredo Codona, who, in a rare schedule
conflict, was not in the Copenhagen circus arena when a swivel
snapped and sent his aerialist wife, Lillian, plummeting to the
ground. At her bedside, where she lingered for a few days
before she died, Alfredo kept blaming himself that he had not
been there to break the fall.

It is true that our friend is always present to our interior
spirit. This is behind Saint-Exupéry's remark that the beacon
light of friendship does not measure our distance from our
friend who is away on a trip but rather beams his or her
continuing presence. Yet our word of friendship means that we
*would* be with our friends at those crucial moments when they
search, even from their sick beds, for our reassuring profile. Just
before she died of heart failure at the age of sixty-two, Jeanette
MacDonald, who had sung of belonging in so many movies from
*Rose Marie* to *Maytime*, emerged from heavy slumber to rest her
eyes upon her husband, Gene Raymond, who was seated next to
her hospital bed. Her eyes were misty as she whispered to him,
"I love you"—and, then, with a quiet serenity "smiling through"
her lovely countenance, she slipped away. No film of hers ever
approached this supreme moment in belonging with her identifying friend. On their wedding day the couple had consecrated
their union with reciprocal words of friendship that proclaimed,
"You are my identifying friend always." From then on they were
never out of each other's interior presence as they strengthened

their bond with each new action of "care for you." Jeanette's final words were much more than a familiar line from the songs she had sung; they were the signature of her total dedication, sacrifice, and gift. The morality of friendship comes into focus in the mutual "I do" of spouses that matures in creative variations of "care for you" in enduring and endearing relationship.

## Covenant of Marriage

Friendship like this could never be programmed! For the morality of friendship is no more a matter of rule than marriage is a mere contract. To characterize marriage as a legal arrangement in which each member exchanges rights and duties falls far short of the reality of friendship. A contract implies no union at all; each party enters into the association "fifty-fifty," for certain reciprocal benefits. The flaw in this contract model of marriage is that it could be defining an invisible line dividing the relationship, thereby making individual considerations paramount. This institutional description of marriage suffers from the Stoic influence that would justify even the most intimate personal bond only in terms of an a priori rational principle.

John Macmurray unmasks the rigid formalism of this parody of Christian morality:

> What Jesus did was to substitute an inner and emotional basis of behaviour for an external and intellectual one. It was the externality of the Pharisee morality which he condemned. And his basis for morality was not rules, principles or laws, but love. And love is emotional, not intellectual... The true Christian morality will be quite different from our orthodox one in its basis and outlook. It will be emotional and in terms of love; not intellectual and in terms of purposes and principles.[6]

It is the *covenant* relationship mentioned in Ephesians that properly describes Christian marriage and the personal morality of love that proves its interior dynamic: "Husbands, love your wives as Christ loved the Church and gave himself for her" (Eph 5:25).

Keeping one's word as friend is a matter of love, not law— as much in marriage as in any bond of close relationship. *Being present* to your spouse as the person who is your identifying friend means that she or he is never left out or kept in the background. The exchange of wedding bands during the ceremony symbolizes this interior identification with one another. Bride Elizabeth and groom William have become one, and their oneness is reflected in the smiling faces of their friends, family, and priest at this glad turning point in their lives. From this day forward, for William to be William is to be in the presence of Elizabeth; for Elizabeth to be Elizabeth is to be in the presence of William. Each is the center of the other's total dedication, care, and concern. The free flow of their mutual communication rests upon the unreserved trust that comes to fulfillment in this shared commitment. In the hush before the altar, the bride and groom have given their word of loyal and persevering friendship. This is the grand meeting in which all the paths of their history converge and in which their separate aspirations combine in their quest for personal fulfillment. The wedding guests follow their smiling faces, turned toward each other almost shyly, as if to avoid the least touch of pressure in this hour of complete spontaneity. Their reciprocal choice, just expressed in the age-old formula, exults in this rare moment of the total outpouring of that special spirit of love, unique with each person, which is now afforded full release in the gracious receptivity of the friend whom he greets for the first time as his bride and she as her husband. In the pause while the organist plays their chosen song, their bliss enfolds all those present, recalling Chaucer's lyric for the celebration of belonging that is particular to each couple:

> And such a joy is there betwixt them two,
> That, save the joy that lasteth evermo',
> There is none like, that any creature
> Hath seen, or shall, while that the world may dure.[7]

This effusive mood carries over from the church to the reception, where the best man raises his glass, with all the guests following suit, to bless the newlyweds with the toast that the happiness of this day will be theirs always—"May your joys be as deep as the ocean and your sorrows, light as its foam!"

That their marriage will last is the heartfelt wish of all their family and friends, but especially of the bride and groom themselves.

Yet the sobering statistic of the divorce rate in the United States, though it casts no shadow upon their wedding, still is sensed at the edge of the proceedings enough to raise awareness. At least one guest at the reception feels a dark cloud pass across his vision—the sad memory of his "former" marriage that prompts his fervent prayer that this young couple may never know the desolation of divorce. The very uncertainty of their future together poses the paradox inherent in the wedding vows: How can I promise on the day of my marriage that I will be your spouse always, since preserving the marital bond depends as much upon you as upon me? Should you go away to marry another, you would no longer be my spouse, never mind that I have kept my covenant with you. Since being spouse is a mutual reality, if you shear off this identification, then I too can no longer be your spouse, however much I would still want to be. Time was when the bride and groom could unhesitatingly pledge that "You will be my spouse always," because the prevailing mores of Western culture allowed them no other option. European and United States society down through World War I was as steadfast as church and synagogue in prohibiting divorce and remarriage. Even in the years following the armistice, so strong was the moral insistence in the United States upon the permanence of the matrimonial tie that a "Reno divorce" was regarded as a statutory fiction to accommodate the free love escapades of film stars in the Roaring Twenties mold. Their zany behavior stood in marked contrast to that of couples serious about their marriage vows for whom divorce was out of the question, no matter what pressures, trials, or even estrangement might crop up in their lives.

This rigid stance, however, had narrowed the morality of marriage to that of absolute law that paid no heed to the intolerable burdens which crushed in upon the household where love between the spouses had long since expired. There is no longer a home where mutual care has withered and died, whether the cause be alcoholism, sexual waywardness, neurotic

130

temper tantrums, financial irresponsibility, or the deadening round of indifference. Friendship can no more be "organized" to routine, than the love of marriage can be mandated by law.

Now, although the stability of partnership in marriage was sustained down to our own day by the indissolubility of the bond as dictated by civil and canon law, this did not mean that union in belonging between the spouses was also thriving. The durability of marriage maintained by statute did enjoy this benefit, however, that neither spouse went packing with the first spat. But even today when divorce and remarriage are readily available, spouses who are intent upon making their marriage work do not go off to their parents the minute a clash occurs in their relationship. There is no denying, though, that if there were only one "go" at marriage in one's lifetime, a person would be extremely careful to make the right choice and to exert every effort to bring the promises of the wedding day to peaceful fulfillment. The motivation for deepening marital friendship is, nevertheless, love—not law—and remains so whether a second marriage is a legal possibility or not. The mistresses of Catholic monarchs for whom marriage was indissoluble did no more to preserve the genuine bond of matrimony than do the paramours of married men today. The point is that, whether she be the Madame Pompadour of a French king or the "other woman" of an American business-man, the subtitle reads the same: the husband's love for his wife as identifying friend has drained away. Law may keep spouses under the same roof, but only love will keep them together as friends.

This, indeed, is the word I can say to my spouse without reservation on our wedding day, "You will *always* be my *friend*." I do not give my pledge of friendship lightly. Here in America we call many people "friends" who are actually just acquaintances or at best close associates! But to my spouse, I do summon my inner resources to make that permanent commitment. I can speak these words in complete sincerity, with no qualms, nor with any misgivings about the hazards contributing to the divorce rate in our nation. What draws me to my friend is her inner goodness that has brought me to myself in evoking my own potential for gift and sacrifice. Because of her special interior worth, I do hold her sacred (*sacrum facere*, again); and the time, effort, work, and even anxiety for her well-being that I will expend from now on, will wed me to her in a way that will never be without significance. This is what Saint-Exupéry means when he says in the words of the little prince's fox, "It is the time that you waste upon your rose that makes your rose so important."[8] Friendship is formed only after utilitarian considerations are laid aside. You give all for your friend because the bond of belonging is priceless, is precious. You belong only to the one for whom you sacrifice. If you sacrifice for no one, you belong to no one. This, in a real sense, is the indissoluble side of matrimony—the marital sacrifice that weaves the bond of belonging. In this reciprocity, in which the spouses give themselves to the other at the same instant in which they receive the gift from the other that lets each fully *be* as a person, strands are woven into the cord of relationship that time cannot diminish, and not even subsequent divorce can empty of significance. The giving of oneself to another in total friendship, if accepted unreservedly by the spouse, is not a grasping for a sunny interval of closeness to stave off the fog of loneliness; it is, rather, the golden moment of interior enfolding in which the unique spirit of each friend comes to brilliant awareness for being nested in the other's heart where the other's devotion nourishes its *ecstatic* beauty.

Description stumbles here because there are no apt metaphors for the personal spirit, precisely because the spirit is unique to each friend and to the particular relationship they form. Nevertheless, the attention that the bride-to-be gives to every detail of her wedding reflects the special significance that the word of friendship between the spouses carries. The phrases of commitment are the core of the wedding ceremony for which all else is confirmation or embellishment, from flowers to photos, from gowns to cake, from music to minister!

This last-mentioned detail, to include a clergyman as witness and to select a church as the locale for their wedding, is not just sentimental attachment to tradition. It manifests, rather, the sure instinct to enshrine this most solemn event of

132

their life in a setting that will lift their moment of mutual commitment beyond the level of the "everyday." In the quiet of this chapel, where a long procession of couples have made their vows, their own exchange of consent is caught up into a context of continuity and permanence that each spouse firmly hopes will distinguish their union. Their wedding is not just an episode; it is a new blend of "I do's" added to those that have gone before, down through the generations, in this sanctuary of God. The symbol-need here is twofold: to highlight the lasting, ennobling worth of their special union here consecrated and to become aware of the nearness of the fatherly God, who covers the couple with His divine protection—so touchingly portrayed in the old Cuban custom of placing a single shawl over the shoulders of the newly-married couple. In that prayerful pause after the minister pronounces them man and wife, there is a keen sense of presences beyond the couple themselves: the tangible, almost touch-on-shoulder presence of parents and of parents' parents married in this chapel or one like it in their native land; and above all, the felt presence of God as the unseen ground for their mutual gift. The inspiriting focus for their nuptial vows is one another. But the still-center for their mutuality beyond mere partnership is the ever-present God who stirs in the heart of each that sense of being knit to him in all circumstances that frees a person for total gift to one's spouse.

This is not just a pious sentiment, dutifully serving the occasion. The constant nearness of God furnishes that reassurance in belonging that is the ever-present yearning of the human spirit. Since this interior peace in relationship is never in jeopardy because of the abiding bond with God, the husband will not manipulate his spouse to fill in those recurring gaps of loneliness that are the vulnerable side of our individual personalities. He will not cling to his wife possessively for fear of being out of her company and left desolate to himself. His spouse can never double for God in his regard, for there is no way that she could possibly fathom those cavernous spaces in his solitude that are a mystery even to himself. There are utterings that come from a restlessness in the depths of his

133

heart—those stirrings known to saint and sinner but not to the mediocre—that only divine responsiveness can assuage. So it is that this prayerful appreciation of the divine presence at the core of your friendship really frees you to say to your spouse on your wedding day, "You will be my friend always." Your own personal realization is never threatened but it reaches for new possibilities of fulfillment in the marriage union.

You each respect the other's privacy and are not dismayed by your spouse's occasional edginess, pensiveness, or mood-swings. You are aware yourself that there are vague depressions that can weigh in on you at times, which you are reluctant to speak about even to that dearest friend sitting across from you at breakfast. Mercifully, your marriage dedication does not rise or fall according to your spouse's emotional climate. Your inner serenity is not clouded by her silent preoccupation with what is bothering her, but has you attend to her all the more. As friend, as husband, as wife, you each have developed a delicate sensitivity to when your spouse craves your company, or perhaps a Sunday drive away from the bin of her anxieties, and especially when her most urgent longing is for the company of no one but her God.

You love your spouse for herself, and you do not insist that every worry upon her mind should pass under your scrutiny. The beauty of friendship, within or outside of marriage, is that it respects the friend's silences as part of the expansive trust that is at the core of any relationship. You have each given yourself away to the other, and in your gift you back away at times to let your spouse hollow out the space she may just then be seeking, simply to be true to her innermost spirit. Such retreat into the core of one's being, in clearing away the clutter of everyday claims, helps a person recover the interior tranquillity which too frantic a pace may have been disturbing. Your spouse's visit to the wellsprings of her personal spirit serves to revitalize her characteristic 'elan' which may have been flagging.

Your union also takes on new richness from the enthusiasm generated by your spouse's individual interests, even though these should take you out of one another's company for brief spells. Conjugal devotion rejoices in the particular accomplishments of a husband or wife. The husband's expert trim-tacking in the annual regatta gladdens his wife; and he heads home to admire the most recent photographic prints that are his wife's absorbing craft. Neither begrudges the other the time these avocations consume because they keep fresh breezes flowing through their union. This supportive atmosphere in the home makes each day an opportunity for enhanced participation. They are so taken up with delight in their combined interests that they would forget to eat, were the children to let them, or if the wife's talents did not run to pie!

If you truly love a person, you set her free to be herself. You can bring this off if you have discovered that profound peace in relationship that doesn't require the wife to be serving up tea or mixing a gin-and-tonic at your every return, to reinforce a feeling of being attended to. The least pious groom that has ever led his bride to the altar, *knows* that in and through his deep down belonging to God he can be a genuine friend to his wife and not hem her in with those demands of oversensitivity that can unravel a marriage. His word of friendship keeps him near, even when his wife's company turns nettlesome. He will stand by to help her through those difficult times when she may be more of a burden to herself than to him. He will not "abandon" her on the excuse of a backlog of work at the office or use some other ploy to stay away. Careful to avoid these small desertions, his inner integrity maintains a lifestyle that avoids the detours that can lead him away from his wife, toward separation or divorce.

## Crisis of Divorce

However, the severest shock that could come to his pledge of marital friendship would be his spouse's sudden announcement that she wants a divorce. Reeling from this unexpected blow, he is under almost insurmountable pressure to turn bitter. Seeing all that he had set his heart upon and worked for go to pieces in this devastating decision of hers tests the strength of his friendship with her. Summoning all his inner reserves, he begins to arrange for the separation, if this is what his spouse feels is most urgent for her happiness and satisfaction. This supportiveness under extreme duress is his way of adhering to his commitment of friendship. Even as the divorce becomes final, he will not cave into the hatred which would be a denial of what he himself has stood for in her regard. This testifies to the maturity of his character as he helps her find herself, even though it be at the cost of the union with her that had been the dearest blessing in his own history. He will not exclude her as friend even when his life with her as spouse comes to a desolating halt. It is at this juncture in his life that his basic tie with God becomes a source of equanimity at the core of his being. This soothing restorative for his bruised spirit urges him to look after his responsibilities to his children without alienating them from their mother. Since their home is broken, they need to tap the reservoirs of his active kindness all the more.

## Responsive Parenting

The children—this is still another dimension implicit in the husband and wife's commitment to friendship on their marriage day. In the Christian marriage ceremony the spouses are explicit about their receptivity to the children that may be born of their union. This openness harmonizes with the Jewish tradition that considers being with child a divine blessing. Unfortunately, the vestiges of Saint Augustine's Manichaean background distorted the Christian view of matrimony in making the procreation of children overshadow the loving union of the spouses as the primary purpose of marriage. The very terminology that could speak of "purpose" rather than "covenant" in describing the marriage relationship smacks more of a Stoic ethical principle "justifying" conjugal intimacy (which, in Augustine's Manichaean-warped outlook, was inherently prone to sin) than of Christian love. But listen again to the pertinent passage in Ephesians:

> Husbands, love your wives as Christ loved the church and gave himself up for it, to consecrate it, cleansing it by water and word, so that he might present the church to himself all glorious, with no stain or wrinkle or anything of the sort, but holy and without blemish. In the same way men also are

bound to love their wives, as they love their own bodies. In loving his wife a man loves himself. For no one ever hated his own body: on the contrary, he provides and cares for it; and that is how Christ treats the church, because it is his body, of which we are living parts. Thus it is that (in the words of Scripture) "a man shall leave his father and mother and shall be joined to his wife, and the two shall become a single body." It is a great truth that is hidden here. I for my part refer it to Christ and to the church, but it applies also individually: each of you must love his wife as his very self; and the woman must see to it that she pays her husband all respect (Eph 5:25–33).

No trace of Manichaeanism or Stoicism here. Rather than disdaining the conjugal expression proper to marriage, this passage endows this specific symbol of marital union with sacramental significance. In our own time the Second Vatican Council has, at long last, restored the balance in concentrating upon the union of the spouses as the very center from which the Christian meaning and morality of matrimony emanates.[9]

The responsible decision of a husband and wife to have a child of their own is an extension of their love for one another. Their commitment to each other in a "covenant" relationship of mutual gift is the foundation of their family planning. Thanks to modern scientific research, there are effective methods which enable a married couple to determine the times best suited for them to conceive children. Providentially, the controversy surrounding contraceptive practice has subsided to a large degree in the wake of mature ethical and theological discussion of the question.

This investigation has made it clear that the same morality of charity that supports organic transplant as commendable action has its application in marriage. The modulation of a biological function, even that of human reproduction, for the good of the spouse, the good of their union, or the well-being and education of the children born of the union, serves the integrity of conjugal charity. From this perspective the morality of married love no longer takes its designation from the subpersonal teleology of the generative process but from the human vision of personal growth in marriage and family. These developing insights, freed from the trappings of an inadequate logic of law, relieve the quandary that had constrained Christian spouses for far too long: the pressure to abstain from the conjugal expression of their married love out of regard for their inability to have a baby because of their economic circumstances or the wife's uncertain health. It was nearly an unchristian irony that the supreme gesture of marital intimacy intended to reinforce the mutual love that was under constant claim of the children already born to them should have been closed off. These spouses, already assuming the considerable task of raising several children, should never have been forbidden the supportive embrace of marital love modulated to prevent further conception. Unhappily, the couple was confronted with an inflexible "Christian" morality of marriage which was in effect a Stoic ethic of natural law, highly tinged with Manichaeanism.

The inner contradiction was that the human values in marriage were made to subserve a bodily function whose interruption was proscribed. The Stoic-Manichaean inversion of Christian morality that insisted upon openness to procreation as the "redeeming" feature in marital intimacy had actually made the personal norms of marriage hinge upon the inviolability of a biological function! This aberration has at long last been unmasked so that the mandate of charity can now hold sway within Christian marriage. The good of the spouse, the strength of their union, and the well-being of the children already in the family are the benchmarks for conjugal morality. This "care for you" will modulate the exercise of the procreative function according to these guidelines.

Moreover, it is the same word of friendship that is sensitive to the needs of husband or wife that supports the yearning of the spouse to introduce a child into their relationship as an extension of their married love. What you love about your spouse is his or her characteristic way of going out to others in interest and love. This is the unique spirit within your spouse that had drawn you together in the first place and had formed the basis of your marital commitment. To restrict this loving spirit in your spouse that longs to welcome a child into your union as the focus of your shared dedication would be to go back on your word of friendship. To choke off the elan of love that is the lifeforce of your conjugal bond cannot but stifle the growth of your friendship. That is the "contraceptive mentality" which can stunt the growth of a marriage. The mutual devotedness involved in the bearing, birth, and education of a child is an invitation to sacrifice. And that sacrifice forms the core of any lasting relationship. You belong only to those for whom you sacrifice! A child born into a union and nurtured to young adulthood stands as a sure witness to parental dedication, the significance of which can never be lost.

The quiet splendor of welcoming children into the family shines forth in contrast to the widespread practice of abortion-on-demand in the United States. But in the confusion brought on by opposing political and social forces in the dreadful debate about abortion, two considerations keep the issues clear. The first is diagnostic: the advanced state of medical science in the United States today puts away any notion that one million abortions per year are medically indicated! The second consideration is conjugal: if a child is conceived in love, whether in or out of wedlock, that child belongs to the relationship always, and consequently has a claim on the care of the parents. True, in the United States the mother or father may insist upon an abortion and legally cut short the life of their child. But the unborn child is still and ever tied to their responsible union, which is personal not biological! Unfortunately, those family planning agencies that suggest contraception and abortion as equally acceptable birth control procedures show little regard for the presence of an unborn human in the womb of the mother. Mercifully, their influence in our society is kept in check by those noble parents who stand by the child of their union, no matter what the sacrifice.

This selfless generosity, in tapping the combined resources of husband and wife, opens fresh paths for the enrichment of their own relationship, unless conflict should arise under the strain of an expanding family. It is probably not too much to say that the authentic test of married love turns upon the parental dimension. Just in the incursions upon one's time that proper child-rearing involves, the mature love of the spouses for one another is put to the test. It is this total sharing, summoned forth when conjugal devotion flowers into family, that led John Macmurray to acclaim that the family "is our only religious institution and it is called upon to do the whole gigantic task of integrating persons in a love unity which is not merely ideal but concrete and creative."[10]

Certainly the tasks that go with parenting are as insistent and as worrisome as ever, even in terms of affording a house. Post-World War II America has also made the automobile a practical necessity for food shopping, church going, and family gatherings for most of the population. The train and trolley fares of former times were much less expensive than financing a car. Getting around took more time; but it was nice to be able to walk to school and stop by the grocery on the way home. Supermarkets today let us stuff our refrigerators with ready-to-cook edibles. In the exchange, however, we now spend our time in checkout lines. Are we ahead? In many ways, surely! But perhaps not so much in available time together.

The working mother certainly appreciates the convenience of quick fixings for dinner. She has had to take a job outside the home to help pay the children's tuition. Her husband's salary cannot keep pace with the rising costs of higher education. This is merely the latest burden imposed upon parents in the United States—the need to assist their young in getting a college education. Time was when the high school graduate would take up a trade or help his dad in the store or on the farm. Those who wanted to go to college would work a year or two to earn the tuition. But the college diploma in those days was not a prerequisite for ample employment opportunity that it is today. Parents intent upon preparing their children to make their way in the world are naturally eager to help them get their Bachelor's degrees. Yet for many a couple, their combined paychecks cannot meet this added expense to their monthly bills. For all their efforts, they may be left with a creeping sense of inadequacy.

This is the extra stress put upon married couples in the

United States today, so paradoxical in our most affluent society. Keeping one's word as friend now has the new challenge of relieving this sense of not measuring up that could easily bear down upon one's spouse. The fact is that, other than a vague, cultural pressure, there is no solid basis for this uneasiness. Nothing in their marriage vows made their covenant hinge upon the size of their take-home pay. Nor was there any promise set down that all good parents must meet the college tuition requirements of their offspring. The truth is that theirs is a working love for their children, lending support as far as their financial capacities allow. The quality of this complete dedication is in no way diminished because a shrinking salary cannot sustain the high cost of college.

## Gracious Caring

This frank recognition of your spouse's limits in being able to provide for the economic needs of the family is one aspect of the perceptive kindness you have for your identifying friend. The same affirmation of your bride or groom that exclaims, "You're so beautiful—look at the way you look at me!"[11] is also keenly aware of the "defect of the quality," as the Irish say. Dealing with your spouse's shortcomings is the way of charity, as John Macmurray reminds: "If you love a person, you love him or her in their stark reality and refuse to shut your eyes to their defects and errors. For to do that is to shut your eyes to their needs."[12]

In the all-encompassing realism of your commitment, your loving glance will not contract to the cold, isolating stare of criticism. After all, you know your spouse's faults better than anyone else, for he has confided them all to you. You have heard all his complaints, especially those he would not dare to express at the office. Your ear has been bent in furnishing the ease of release for the discouraging wounds to his heart.

On the other had, his modesty is slow to tell you about his accomplishments for the company. You know him so well that he doesn't want to "blow his own horn," though he will allow you a glimpse of the glow that an upturn at work has brought to his inner spirit. He lets you in on his laurels to rejoice your heart, not to impress you with the "kind of guy" you espoused. In his "down" hours he seeks the comfort of your sympathetic presence. In his grand moments he is almost child-shy about recounting his success. He knows that you love him, whether he ever brings home a ribbon or not. So he is slow to let a trophy of his clutter the mantel he reserves for photos of you and the children.

This is the paradox of married friendship, that the spouse's finest hours often transpire beyond the notice of the beloved: the husband's deft diplomacy in defusing a labor dispute at the office; the wife's quiet anticipation of the needs of a new neighbor whose husband has suddenly been taken to hospital. Yet the failings of the spouse seem to crop up at every turn, as if they were meant to be the private preserve of husband or wife. Each seems to be entrusted with the shortcomings in the other that escape public notice, almost as a confided secret. Consequently, to flail a spouse for these hidden flaws amounts to a kind of infidelity, because the scolding excludes a person within his own home! What "out" is there, since in terms of their identifying relationship each is all the other has.

In their intramural skirmishes, each spouse is sure of the mark, once their disagreement has degenerated into fault-finding. There is no defense that either can mount against this tirade. Our individual characteristics actually make up our personhood. Thus a high-strung person, for instance, can hardly become otherwise without becoming unstrung! Clinkers nestle beneath diamonds in the mine of personality, so that cherishing the irreplaceable worth in your spouse transforms the clay in you both—"Only the spirit, if it breathe upon the clay, can create the person"—[13] the spirit, that is, of compassionate gratefulness for that someone who made the uncommon choice of dedicating his or her life to you!

Another form of criticism that undermines the integrity of one's conjugal friendship is sniping at the parents, relatives, and friends of the spouse. To test the wider loyalties of a husband or wife in this way is sure to put the spouse on the defensive. On their marriage day the couple initiated their own identifying relationship that takes priority over all other bonds, except the

142

tie to God that is the ground of stability for their union. This precedence should probably be emphasized in every marriage ceremony since many parents are not quite prepared for the transition that takes son or daughter out of the household. Nevertheless, forestalling interference from in-laws begins with a genuine respect for one another's family and friends that reinforces the all-embracing regard a person holds for husband or wife.

Her family and friends had long ago called forth those engaging qualities in your wife that warm your heart and make you rejoice in her companionship. Your ungrudging welcome for her acquaintances allows her to sort out and recognize those true friendships that will stay with her always. A winnowing occurs when the bride and groom cross the threshold into married life that makes all the previous skittishness about who will be in the bridal party seem unimportant. Whatever became of the bridesmaids of yesteryear? They were the girlhood chums who walked in colorful procession, leading your bride to quite another life that leaves most of them behind in fond but dimming memory. A few do keep close. Hopefully then, the love of a man for his bride (and of a woman for her husband) is secure enough to ride with the tides of human association and not resent the spouse's delight in being with those abiding friends who inhabit a corner of her heart.

This steady equanimity presumes a profound respect for your spouse that is reflected in the gentle language you use to converse with one another, even when you strongly disagree about something. Here we come to the two prerequisites for an enduring relationship without which your word of friendship will wear thin and collapse. The first is the undiminished appreciation for the unique worth of your spouse. Self-serving preoccupations must be kept from insinuating themselves into the relationship. For if the day ever arrives when a spouse feels that she is being used by her husband, or vice versa, the marital bond is already on the verge of snapping. Exploitation in marriage is another form of infidelity that makes a mockery of conjugal friendship. The egocentric utilitarianism of our age is so much a part of our cultural context that it can easily make inroads into the best of marriages. Fortunately, there is an honesty and integrity about true friendship that is alert to this peril and, early on, exposes its cunning approaches.

The other prerequisite for enhancing the vigor of the wedding bond is not achieved overnight. This is graciousness of language in conversing with one's spouse. There are many ways of dealing with people that mirror our respect, and the most important of these is our manner of speech. Catch the sound of your voice and listen for those phrases that frequently fall from your lips, and you will have a sampling of the talk that cascades upon your spouse day-in and day-out through your years together. Of course, there is little we can do about the particular pitch of our voice. But there is everything we can do about molding habits of speaking that are congenial rather than harsh, soothing rather than strident, and that impart peace rather than discord.

Being unpracticed in the gentle ways of speaking leaves us with nothing but the bludgeons of the vulgar vernacular when we become extremely angry with our spouse. Words become weapons then, and our cutting language may cause greater hurt than the issue that caused the dispute in the first place. We interpret ourselves to one another through our ways of speaking. Yet these are the ingredients of friendship that have suffered dire neglect in modern American schooling. The Killarney cattle drover who left the classroom at twelve to mind the farm has a delicacy of language that outshines that of the American high school graduate whose parlance was fashioned in the curious mix of television's Maude, Archie Bunker, and "Three's Company."

It is a pity that, when disagreements erupt amongst the best of friends, there is a paltry store of civilized talk with which to mend the frayed relationship. Temper, drink, and erratic behavior can all take their toll in wearing down a friendship, especially in marriage. But a failure in considerate language is most regrettable because it does not indicate a flaw in character but rather a serious shortcoming in self-presentation. Words can wound, and vulgarity evokes vulgarity so that the inherent nobility in marital friendship is tarnished. Spouses find their proper image in one another. But if the mirror is muddied, the vision is blurred if not distorted. A breach in graciousness can shut out a spouse more effectively than any other single factor, because there is no welcome without gentility. The carping wife can catapult a husband to the race track or pub. The coarse-mouthed husband can push his wife off to the haven of flea-marketing, church suppers, or to the duties of looking after the children with a minimum of parental dialogue.

This breakdown in the word of friendship comes about when the serene conversation that is the hallmark of the conjugal bond fails. The violence of rough language boxes out the identifying friend and may even tempt the injured spouse to seek comfort in extramarital companionship. The latter is properly called marital infidelity. But the verbal exchanges between the spouses that seared their relationship down to its last strand constituted a prior "infidelity" that had deprived one or both spouses of an essential sense of belonging.

Adultery, nonetheless, for all its media depiction that might have us believe it unavoidable, is a grave infidelity that strikes at the heart of matrimony. For no matter what the circumstances that may have led to it, adultery is a betrayal. It is a going back on one's word of care for the spouse as identifying friend. Since time immemorial, the specific symbol for conjugal unity has been the sexual union of the spouses; and it remains so, even in the face of today's "emancipated" moral trends. Consequently when a man makes love to a woman other than his wife, through this symbolic action he is excluding his spouse in this moment of personal intimacy. This is the sin of it—the breaking of his word as spouse. It is as if he were hurling this message at his wife: "You are my identifying friend, but not just now." This double-talk doesn't wash, since true union with one's spouse does not suffer gaps or interruptions, ever! The exclusion of the spouse as identifying friend in the marital action symbolic of their conjugal bond is the intrinsic contradiction that makes adultery such an affront to married love. Mutual meanings are sheared away in the extramarital excursion.

The glaring evidence is in the hurt! Adultery wounds. The biting edge of the injury is in being turned aside for another.

145

This is the dishonesty that slices through the whole fabric of the marriage union. In the aftermath, reciprocal trust between the spouses is severely harmed. And since this openness of complete confidence in the spouse is at the vital center of conjugal life and love, adultery is the one sin that must not be committed the first time. The adulterous husband, for example, has put himself in a bind: If he admits his extramarital intimacy with another, his wife will be stunned, shaken, cut to the heart, so that her trust in him can never be quite the same. Yet if he keeps this sorry episode from her, he has already compromised the total and unreserved communication they had enjoyed with one another up until then. Either way, the uninhibited quality of their spontaneous trust in one another is badly damaged. And though forgiveness and reconciliation mercifully take place, the scars remain. In spite of the modern talk of "freedom" in marriage, the blow dealt by adultery in its trampling upon mutual trust is a falling away from a covenant with a friend. The disloyalty cannot be treated casually without implicitly denying the dignity of the spouse and any substantial worth to one's commitments. Keeping one's word as friend is the core of "care for you," both in and outside of marriage.

The integrity of the love of friendship is reflected in the totally dedicated married couple. The reciprocity of their selfless commitment is repeated in every genuine relationship of belonging. Can this also be said of the couple who choose to live together without the seal of matrimony? Certainly the oft-stated claim of these couples is that the boundless quality of their love far outreaches the need for the "piece of paper" that is the marriage certificate. However, they always add another reason to justify their alliance: that it is better to experience firsthand how they will mate and get along together without risking the distress of divorce.

A slight discrepancy already blurs their clear avowal. For if, in fact, their mutual love goes beyond the need for a marriage ceremony, there could hardly be a need to verify its durability in a trial run. The hitch is that it is almost impossible to test the permanence of a conjugal tie in the context of a relationship that is inherently provisional. Either party could pack up and leave on the morrow with no strings attached. In view of this possiblility, one or both of the parties may be quite solicitous to be a tidy, pleasant, nonbothersome companion in order to insure that the congenial rapport of their association might evolve into an enduring bond. Such an apprenticeship, however, is futile since friendship, especially married friendship, can never be merited or earned. Organizational logic falters before the spontaneity and totality of interpersonal love.

This is not to question the sincere devotion that initiated the couple's pact to live together. The presumption is that they both truly love one another for the sake of the other! Otherwise their arrangement would simply be one of reciprocal self-interest with sexual gratification a dominant motif. The second presumption is that the choice is prompted by unpressured devotedness. If the girl, for instance, accedes to her boyfriend's insistence that she move in with him out of an uneasiness about losing his friendship, her decision turns more upon fear than upon full, trusting love.

The couple here, however, have made a completely free decision to live in a conjugal way outside marriage. The pivotal question for them, then, is this: Could their living together be a violation of their reciprocal word of care that is the foundation of their relationship? The answer is yes, if it brings harm to either of the friends. This becomes the situation if their living together sows anxiety, say, in the girl that the permanent union symbolized in their lifestyle—as if husband and wife—may never come about. Their intimate association raises the hope of a lasting bond with no firm assurance that it will be more than a passing episode. The yearning for permanence stirred in their conjugal mode of living is dampened in the awareness that there has been no espousal. This is the distress that a dedicated friend would not impose upon his beloved.

Moreover, in his sensitive regard for her special beauty as a person, he would not want to give the slightest hint that she does not deserve the total commitment of matrimony. The sincerity of his affection for her would balk at downgrading her own sense of worth by suggesting that she live with him outside marriage—as if she could expect no better! In his own inner integrity, he cannot invite her to conjugal intimacy without the marital commitment that instills within them both the stability of assured belonging. Until he makes this sacrifice for her, and she for him, they are still just two individuals nestled together with the realization of genuine conjugal belonging ever beyond their reach.

Sincerity, respect, sacrifice—these are the gracious qualities with which the person of integrity endows all friendship. If you love someone as friend, you cannot treat him or her in a shabby manner without betraying your own intrinsic worth as a person. This is the note which John Macmurray used to close his BBC radio series over fifty years ago: "Moral conduct *is* beautiful conduct . . . Nothing that is not inherently beautiful is really good . . . It is vulgarity that is the matter with us— particularly the vulgarity of our moral ideas."[14] Keeping our word as friend is the interior principle enkindling the warmth of relationship that is the one lasting beauty in the personal world.

## Expansive Care

This same "beautiful" word of care, with its deep-seated respect for all people, extends to persons we do not know. The ugliest blotch on the modern scene is the violence laid upon strangers in our society. The muggings, commercial cheating, stealing, sexual assaults, physical injury, and death visited upon these innocents in our cities is an assault upon all it means to be human. Even the ease with which abortion is promoted in our society would present the unborn child as still another "stranger" in our midst.

Insisting upon respect for the anonymous "other" in our society is inseparable from our word of care for our friends. That stranger could be my child or my brother trying to find his way in unfamiliar surroundings. That unborn child is trying to get a hold on human life, the same way I once did, and deserves the same *humane* attention. Reassuringly, the New Jersey truck driver who risked the flames to pull the Chinese couple from their burning auto was marvelously humane in his spontaneous care for the unknown Orientals.

But perhaps in the end, the morality of "care for you" that is so constricted in our time with regard to strangers will prevail once again only in the recovery of the religious perspective. From this vantage point, we can remind ourselves that the lonely veteran sitting in the all-night cafe sipping coffee takes his interior dignity from the same source of personal spirit as I. The Puerto-Rican woman in Spanish Harlem—widowed when her young husband went down in a street stabbing—who is doing her best to raise her *niños*, two boys and a girl, prays to the same God as I. Blessedly, the rolling sounds of her *Padre Nuestro* were lifted to heaven from our American shores long before the "Our Father" was invoked by our colonial pioneers.

The word of care needs a return of the word of prayer in our land so that we will again come to realize that the stranger we welcome and respect is linked to the divine Son, who had said, "Whatever you did to one of these, the least of my brethren, you did to me" (Mt 25:40). Then the beauty of friendship, shaped in the integrating morality of care for you, will encompass all others, neighbors and strangers alike, as members of that same family for whose oneness Jesus had prayed at the last: "O Father, may they all be one, as Thou, Father, are in me and I in Thee: may they be one in us!"(Jn 17:21) There are no strangers in the family of the Father—only brothers and sisters we haven't yet had the chance to meet.

# EIGHT

## *The Celebration of Belonging*

We humans mark our milestones with symbol and ceremony. We want to capture the special significance of our
deepest hopes and aspirations in appropriate imagery. Symbol
and ceremony are the concrete expression of the importance we
attach to the values that bind our time, energy, and heart. We
simply will not let the priceless moments in the lives of those so
dear to our heart slip by without a sign of glad appreciation.

The christening of our youngest daughter calls for sublime
ceremony and vibrant imagery to announce the entrance of this
tiny bundle of uniqueness into the human family of God. And
when, all too soon, this precious daughter of ours finishes
college, it will not do for the dean merely to mail the diploma.
Not at all! The procession must be formed so all can see the
graduates march by in academic gown and mortar-board,
bearing the hood and colors of their baccalaureate. "And the one
with the shy smile and gentle blue eyes—her father's eyes—the
tall girl there with brunette bangs crossing her forehead—that's

151

our daughter Nettie. You can't miss her, but then we see her in a special way that her graduation portrait doesn't even hint at. For us, there is only one person in the line of march, and tears blur our vision now because we're bursting with pride for her and wonder how it is that God our Father should ever have blessed us with the presence of such a loving person. Oh, she's no wilting violet, understand, but her innate goodness and quiet compassion for others have reassured us with a touch of God's own love in our lives. Nettie, it *is* a fine day!"

These are the reflections on the unique worth and beauty of a person that a campus rite like graduation or church rites like baptism and marriage stir. Ceremony halts the humdrum of the everyday to call attention! Whether the Archbishop of Canterbury be anointing the second Elizabeth as queen of England or a local pastor be crossing the baptismal chrism on an Alsace couple's newborn daughter, Marlyse (Mary Elizabeth), we would raise this moment beyond the encroachments of daily routine. We stay the tide of pressing business to proclaim: "This person is very special to us and we shall not see her like ever again. So let us cherish her priceless moment of commencement!"

The striking feature here is that nearly all of our symbolism looks forward, as it highlights a new venture, a setting forth, a *commencement*. If Heinrich Boll, the late West German novelist, can say, "We're born to remember; that's what we're here for," the ceremony enshrines a key event in our memory precisely so that we can move down through our future history in the invigorating significance of this moment. From the pinning of nurses to the oathing of presidents, we are launching the man or woman "of the hour" upon a course in which each takes up a new identity and fresh responsibility. This surely accounts for our natural inclination to shower these occasions with sparkling jubilation. We would hope that the honored persons keep the joyful glow of their special day to see them through those dark times when crushing burdens or dull drudgery begin to take their toll.

Mere external trappings, of course, cannot move the spirit. But crisp, impressive ceremonial, in calling forth prayerful congratulation from a parent or the smiling enthusiasm of one's closest friend suffuses the heart with the inner meaning of the event. It was the flicker of just such a "call to honor" upon his St.-Cyr graduation that flamed to brilliance on that fateful June 18th, 1940, when little-known Charles de Gaulle became the rallying voice for a prostrate France. The still-gleam at the core of de Gaulle's character diffused itself as the beacon light of courage for countrymen like François Mauriac, who describes its transfiguring impact:

> We, during those bitter winter nights, kept our ears glued to the radio, while the steps of the German officer shook the ceiling overhead. We listened, fists clenched, and did not restrain our tears. We ran to tell the other members of the family: "General de Gaulle is going to speak; he's speaking now.!"[1]

Symbols enlighten; symbols inspire. We cannot dispense with symbol and ceremony without obscuring the value of our calling and diminishing our own interior sense of worth. Our keen awareness of the human ideal enshrined within a treasured medal, uniform, or ring springs from our mature self-confidence thrusting for personal dedication. We instinctively set to symbol those deep-down values that can engage one's heart and fill one's life—whether it be Antoine de Saint-Exupéry's squadron badge of Air Group 2/33, or the silver wedding bands exchanged between bride Elizabeth and groom William in the Strasbourg chapel on their wedding day. These symbols reflect the pricelessness of commitment, both in the sterling quality of the covenant that is chosen and in the integrity of the persons making the avowal.

Each of us is an artist shaping the image of the person we are yearning to become. Our inner spirit searches among the various images of human aspiration for an appealing feature to fold into our interior picture of uniqueness. Certain images attract us as we find ourselves blending their characteristics into our emerging profile. Other images we shun as strangely discordant, boring, or even abhorrent to our unspoken sense of what we are about as persons. For in the end, this most personal montage of our uniqueness with which we identify must be inherently beautiful and worthy of us. Otherwise, it will not stir our full enthusiasm for commitment.

This is why we are never quite at ease with the blandishments of affluence. We know that money is the very necessary means for meeting the persistent obligations that come of living in modern society. Nevertheless, we admit, to ourselves at least, that currency carries no intrinsic significance. It is merely common tender. Its very impersonality belies its allure. How wistfully a paycheck conceals the special craftsmanship of a shoemaker, the expertise of a tailor. The dollar sign says little of the skill, toil, and concentrated energies that the artisan put into his product. The price tag allows for a profit-margin which is prerequisite for the upcoming bank loan for new inventory. Nonetheless, to let the heart fix itself on profit for its own sake is to settle for dross. The underpaid dressmaker in the Brooklyn sweat shop keeps her dignity: her artistry is embroidered into the garment she fashions. The profiteer, by contrast, has permitted money and the things it can buy to become the token of his worth, and that is mere casino coin, as common as coal.

Our consumer society, with all of its merchandising techniques, plays an incessant drumbeat upon our purchasing reflexes and would make the pursuit of money—as such—valid as a human quest. Yet the inward sense of our personal integrity keeps us free of that gross entanglement, though, admittedly, it does become increasingly difficult these days to raise the vision of our impressionable young to those precisely human values that far outreach cash considerations. Even more disheartening is the way in which self-gratification is offered to our young people in the guise of being the well-deserved reward for earnest, human effort. Capping a burning oil well calls for a beer, if you would believe an oft-repeated television commercial. As if Michelangelo sculpted his David for the evening assuagement of de Medici wine!

Quenching one's thirst is, indeed, "the pause that refreshes." But Madison Avenue's emphasis upon sensate satisfaction as a goal unto itself is surely an affront to adult maturity. Moreover, when this approach spreads to the enticements of sexual encounter, with erotic indulgence portrayed as part of the "cool," masculine image, veneered vulgarity has come full circle. When persons called to expansive living in the full potential of their special gift tie their dreams to the sexual fantasies of *Playboy* magazine, the closing down of their cherished horizons of inner expectation can leave them with a glum emptiness. Neither well-heeled greed nor modish lust have ever completely rejoiced the human heart, for all their glamorous deployment in our time. Mercifully, the conviction of our intrinsic worth can never be totally snuffed out; a tiny spark always flickers deep within us as the faint symbol of our special nobility, summoning yet another fresh surge from our unique spirit.

Almost instinctively we look to our poets and singers to enkindle this flame of grand aspiration, as once upon a time "the singer began to sing over the rocking cradle or among the wine-cups, and it was though life itself caught fire of a sudden."[2] William Butler Yeats is here extolling the lyric word, especially when set to music, as the supreme mode of expressing "my dreams of your image that blossoms a rose in the deeps of my heart."[3] Yes, we do mirror ourselves in others; and from our earliest years we identified ourselves by the word-designations we assimilated from parent, brother or sister, schoolmate or teacher. Then, all too soon, those awkward, probing teenage years loomed when we attempted our first solo ventures into adult life. It was then that we turned to the charged language of a favorite verse or poster or song that expressed our emerging vision of happiness, along with the aching disappointments that are the flipside of our dreams. Our bulging record cabinets from those years show Yeats to have been right. The Beatles may have been the troubadours of our tentativeness, or perhaps Joni Mitchell was the one to help us "look at life from both sides now." Bing Crosby and Peggy Lee had met this need for an earlier generation, just as John McCormack had put lilt into the lives of bone-weary Irish-American immigrants at the dawn of the Victrola.

Though we are not a singing nation in the manner of our European ancestors, we still delight in the lyric words that voice the deepest yearnings of our heart. Digital recordings may have displaced the living harmonies of hearthside. But a disc or cassette by mezzo-soprano Frederica von Stade, for instance, gives lyrical expression to our profound feelings—whether longing for the beloved in Mozart's aria *"Vedrai carino"* from *Don Giovanni* or rhapsodizing about him in Jerome Kern's song "You Are Love" from *Show Boat*. Of course, in textbook, word processor, or television newscast, the written or spoken word is the ordinary medium for disseminating information. But the lyric word, in contrast, is laden with emotional overtones which resonate directly with the aesthetic fibers at the core of our being. The breathtaking lyricism immediately conveys the exhilaration of the young couple in Bernstein's *West Side Story,* who thrill at the prospect that "somewhere there's a place for us." This phrase of theirs, stripped of emotional connotation, would merely suggest a street address; but infused with the gladness of the music, it transports Maria and her fiancé to the verge of glowing communion.

The apt symbol for our particular vision imparts the joy, the wonder, and the grandeur that bring us together as friends to share its meaning as the fond center of our living. This is why bride and groom are so choosy about the song to be sung at their wedding: it is meant to represent the radiant hopes which they share and which have drawn forth their commitment to one another in the promise of a lifetime together.

The song is symbol of their joy, catching the star-gleam of the wine glass with which they accept the best man's toast to them as husband and wife. In that shining moment, the couple make real Antoine Roger de Saint-Exupéry's most exquisite phrase celebrating the belonging that is true friendship: "we will touch glasses in the peace of your smile, bright as the dawn."[4] The song then forms the measures of the couple's first dance that begins their "celebration of belonging" at the wedding banquet. As they circle the floor, the song of their heart to which they dance becomes the symbol of their mature togetherness. The rhythm of their wedding waltz pulses to the heartbeat of their union in belonging, wherein each completely respects the other in total devotion. Anne Morrow Lindbergh marvelously etches the meaning of this dance in *Gift from the Sea:*

When the heart is flooded with love, there is no room in it
for fear, for doubt, for hesitation. And it is this lack of fear
that makes for the dance, when each partner loves so completely that he has forgotten to ask himself whether or not
he is loved in return.[5]

The lyric spontaneity of total gift that is the gracious
overtone in the spouses' nuptial dance carries over into their
first dinner together as husband and wife. Theirs is a communion in the "breaking of bread," that symbolizes the total
participation that will mark their lives from this day forward.
The bread will be the plain "down home" sign of their labor in
forming family together. Saint-Exupéry delighted in this image
of the wheat of personal communion:

It is true that upon their return home they take the wheat
as nourishment. But, for a person, this is not at all the
important dimension. What nourishes his heart is not what
he takes from the wheat but what he gives to it . . . And if
the taking allows the body to thrive, it is the giving alone
that sustains the heart.[6]

The hidden sustenance of the wedding meal for bride and groom
is the total mutuality of their gift to one another. That is what
makes their communion in the breaking of the bread a true
celebration of belonging, imaging the ardor each will bring to
the wheat of their relationship down through the years.

This marriage banquet was in preparation all through their
previous history. Little did they know as toddlers the import of
their parents' insistence that they offer a portion of their cookie
or cracker to their playmate in the backyard. The tasty snacks
were already seen as offerings to a companion, like the slices of a
birthday cake. Even mealtime manners reinforced this other-
centered intent—to wait until all were served before starting to
eat; to save the last portion for the next family member down
the table; to keep elbows off the table since it was communal,
not anyone's private preserve; not to absent oneself from the
dinner table without the permission of the head of the family.
Through all this they gradually absorbed the notion that the
breaking of bread with friend and family was more than

157

nutritional; it was a rite of belonging—a little space carved out of a busy day in which all the members gathered together to appreciate their bond with one another.

It was only much later that I realized why my own father had been annoyed with me for letting work on a high school newspaper keep me so often from our own family dinner. I was to leave the family circle and go off to college at age eighteen. Sadly, my father was in his grave before I graduated. Our time for sharing had been but brief segments in the span of my years, and I had even squandered some of those in "doing my own thing." In later years and almost as a second chance, my married sister would have me as a guest at her family table, with her husband and ten children. A baker's dozen, we: five boys, five girls, John and Barbara, plus the phantom uncle who came on the scene once or twice a year, like a windblown sailor home from the sea. And we shared bread. Nothing fancy: my sister and brother-in-law's riches were all poured into their family and their three-bedroom home. How I would look forward to the semiannual journey at Christmas and Independence Day to relish the interdependence of family and nourish once again the ties of belonging in holiday dinner and summer cookout. As I would board the plane in Newark for Cleveland, I felt in my bones the lines Saint-Exupéry had written when he, too, was on a homeward leg:

> We fly towards comrades and a kind of celebration. A lamplight gleaming in the humblest hut can change the rudest winter night into Christmas Eve. We in this plane are bound for a place where there will be comrades to welcome us. We in this plane are bound for the communion of our daily bread.[7]

We traveled home to participate in the breaking of bread, not to gourmandize. The vitamins of the spirit are of a different order, as St-Ex had learned from the hardy *paysan* with whom he stayed:

> The farmer handing round the bread had made no gift to us at table: he had shared with us and exchanged with us that bread in which all of us had our part. And by that

sharing, the farmer had not been impoverished but enriched. He had eaten sweeter bread, the bread of community, by that sharing.[8]

Saint-Exupéry thus captures the essence of the sharing in
the wedding banquet of bride and groom. For their previous
involvement in family dinners at Christmas and Easter, Thanksgiving and birthdays, all had been a prelude for this meal. This
supreme celebration of belonging for the married couple is built
upon the meaning of participation that was nurtured in these
"rites of communion" in family and friendship over the years.
Whether it was the fiftieth birthday of a grandmother or the
parents' twenty-fifth wedding anniversary, each ceremonial
brought forth the significance of mutual belonging. Further-
more these events, according to John Macmurray, are inherently religious:

> To grasp the meaning of religion, we must think together
> the occasions on which human beings celebrate their
> fellowship. We must think of two friends who have met
> after a long separation and who say, "Let's go out and
> celebrate"; of a family celebrating the birthday of one of the
> children; as well as of the celebration of Holy Communion
> in a Christian cathedral or village chapel.[9]

The celebration of belonging of the wedded couple is
religious, the wine of their marital toast symboling their
covenant of total love and the bread they break together, the
communion created in their mutual commitment. And yet the
symbolism of their wedding banquet can only be called religious
in the conviction that God, as the source of personal spirit, is the
dynamic center of all genuinely personal relationships. For
every authentic wedding dispels the specter of individualism
that stalks humankind and which John Macmurray considers to
be the denial of the divine in human affairs: "For the great
negation of religion is individualism, egocentricity become a
philosophy; and it is inherently atheist, however much it says
"Lord, Lord!"[10]

Consequently, my commitment to devote my life to you in
unreserved self-donation, which is the essence of what the

spouses promise to one another, is a profoundly religious statement. Perhaps this is why Jesus came to Cana to bless a wedding with the wine of his generosity. This may also be why the marriage banquet would be his favorite image for the kingdom of his Father. Appropriately for the Catholic bride and groom, the significance of their wedding dinner begins in church with the nuptial Mass, where they partake of the bread that is the body of the Lord and drink from the wine cup of the new covenant in his blood. The joys and sorrows that will weave through their married life will be transfigured with lasting meaning because they are linked with the covenant of God's Son in our regard.

But whether the couple seal their vows in the remembrance of the Lord's Supper or in the traditional marriage ceremony, it is their mutual love that makes God present in their union. At that first Eucharist Jesus announced reassuringly, "If a person loves me, he will keep my word, and my Father will love him, and we will come and make our home with him" (Jn 14:23). Jesus had already made that "word" to be kept eminently clear to his friends: "A new commandment I give you, that you love one another even as I have loved you" (Jn 13:34). This is the word the spouses give to each other—to love one another with all their hearts—and their reciprocal love will draw to them the loving presence of the Father and the divine Son who became human in Jesus.

The wedding flowers reflect the joyful exultation and serenity of this beautiful moment when bride and groom leave aside their individual self-concern to fulfill the longings of their unique spirit of gift in total personal union with one another. At this most golden instant in their history, two particular flowers, the rose and the fleur-de-lys, have special meaning for the spouses because they stand for the Lord and for one another in him. The rose represents Jesus as the beloved of the Father; it goes back to Isaiah 11 that speaks of the flower that will bloom on the stem of Jesse. The fleur-de-lys, for its part, symbolizes the flowering of the cross of Calvary and represents the Risen Lord transcending death, as the source of our life and love.

These two flowers in turn symbolize the deeper signifi-

160

cance of the two spouses becoming one in the Lord on their wedding day. The rose stands for bride and groom as the beloved both of the Father and of the divine Son—Saint-Exupéry's prince. The fleur-de-lys as the age-old image of the Lord's resurrection casts its radiance upon all the spouses will share in their life together: it means that whatever husband and wife do in word or work, joy or sorrow for each other and for those entrusted to their care will be caught up in the love of the Son for the Father and will keep forever. The fleur-de-lys stands for a lifetime of love—and the eternal life of belonging to one another in the Risen Jesus that their mutual love will bring. The most obscure couple saying their wedding vows in a quiet chapel constitute the "wedding of the century," because theirs is a celebration of belonging in Christ. There is a "fleur-de-lys" quality about their union that will never disappear, not through the end of time.

Symbols and ceremonial signify our noblest longings and achievements—they have marked our choices at the turning points of our lives. Yet so many of them seem to cluster in our twenties, as they did for John Shea. He was only twenty-one when he graduated from Boston College. He wasn't much older when he was commissioned a lieutenant in the United States Navy, wearing the proud insignia of the crossed anchors on the shield of stars and stripes. John soon took his bride to the altar where they dedicated their lives to one another in vows, rings, flowers, and in the Eucharist of the Lord. At their wedding banquet John and his bride rejoiced in their toast, their first waltz as Mr. and Mrs., and their nuptial dinner, topped off with the cutting of the cake.

The couple had savored those first months of marriage together and were made blissfully happy by the arrival of their firstborn, John Jr. Another ceremonial, that of baptism, enriched their lives as they took on the responsibilities of guiding their son in his first steps on the highway of life. But all too soon the dark clouds of World War II cut across the serenity of their family life, as Commander Shea was assigned to the U.S.S. Wasp for duty in the South Pacific. It was late summer of 1942 when John Shea was able to talk to his wife and son for the last time on a transoceanic telephone. Sensing the ominous danger of an impending sea battle, John sat down to write a few lines to his young son, just in case! Only a few days later Commander Shea went down with his ship and was posthumously awarded the Navy Cross for bravery. His letter enshrines with muted simplicity the lasting meaning behind the symbols that had marked his life and for which he gave his final breath:

Dear Jackie,

This is the first letter I have written directly to my little son. I am thrilled to know you can read it all by yourself. If you miss some of the words it will be because I do not write very plainly. Mother will help you in that case, I am sure.

I was certainly glad to hear your voice over the long distance telephone. It sounded as though I were right in the living room with you. You sounded as though you missed your daddy very much. I miss you, too, more than anyone will ever know. It is too bad this war could not have been delayed a few more years so that I could grow up again with you and do all the things I planned to do when you were old enough to go to school.

I thought how nice it would be to come home early in the afternoon and play ball with you and go mountain climbing and see the trees, brooks, and learn all about woodcraft, hunting, fishing, swimming and other things like that. I suppose we must be brave and put these things off now for a while.

When you are a little bigger you will know why your daddy is not home so much any more. You know we have a big country and we have ideals as to how people should live and enjoy the riches of it and how each is born with equal rights to life, freedom and the pursuit of happiness. Unfortunately, there are some countries in the world where they do not have these ideals, where a boy cannot grow up to be what he wants to be with no limit on his opportunities to be a great man such as a great priest, statesman, doctor, soldier, business man, etc.

Because there are people in countries who want to change our nation, its ideals, its form of government and way of life, we must leave our homes and families to fight.

Fighting for the defense of our country, ideals, homes and honor is an honor and a duty which your daddy has to do before he can come home and settle down with you and mother. When it is done, he is coming home to be with you always and forever. So wait just a little while longer. I am afraid it will be more than the two weeks you told me on the phone.

In the meantime take good care of mother; be a good boy and grow up to be a good young man. Study hard when you go to school. Be a leader in everything good in life. Be a good Catholic and you can't help being a good American. Play fair always. Strive to win; but if you must lose, lose like a gentleman and a good sportsman. Don't ever be a quitter, either in sports or in your business or profession when you grow up. Get all the education you can. Stay close to Mother and follow her advice. Obey her in everything, no matter how you may at times disagree.

She knows what is best and will never let you down or lead you away from the right and honorable things of life. If I don't get back, you will have to be Mother's protector because you will be the only one she has. You must grow up to take my place as well as your own in her life and heart.

Love your grandmother and granddad as long as they live. They, too, will never let you down. Love your aunts and see them as often as you can. Last of all, don't ever forget your daddy. Pray for him to come back and if it is God's will that he does not, be the kind of a boy and man your daddy wants you to be.

Kiss Mother for me every night. Goodby for now. With all my love and devotion for Mother and you,

Your Daddy

The dignity and nobility and poignant beauty of this document need no music to portray the values for which John Shea gave his life. Its lyric quality welled up in his pen from the deep sensitivity of a quiet Celtic sailor who was ready for sacrifice, should God make the call. There is nothing vicarious in the lines of this letter. Their measured cadences come from a man who could hope at all because he took life seriously in resting his dreams in the ineffable designs of a provident God.

163

The fleur-de-lys transcendence of Easter streams through John Shea's letter to his son and through Antoine Roger de Saint-Exupéry's poignant reflection on friendship in his letter to a hostage.

The smile of reunion shines through the words of the sailor and the pilot, who each belong always to their friends and family through their total sacrifice in the war from which neither returned. Somehow the smiles of these men must linger in the hearts of those dear to them, because a person's unique smile is the ultimate symbol of belonging, whether tendered in welcome or good-bye. In a way, Saint-Exupéry wrote his own epitaph, though neither he nor John Shea were to have assigned graves:

> A smile is often essential:
> One is compensated in a smile.
> One is rewarded with a smile.
> One is motivated by a smile.
> And, the quality of a smile is such
> that one could give his very life for it.[11]

The smile of friendship images the eternal bond of belonging. Significantly, the smile of God's friendship is the blessing Moses had implored for the Israelites: "May the Lord bless you and keep you: may he let his face shine upon you" (Nm 6:24). This was the smile that the rich young man had experienced when Jesus "looked upon him and loved him" (Mk 10:21). His is the welcoming smile who promised, "I will come again and receive you to myself" (Jn 14:3). The smiling countenance of the host of the Last Supper is the reassurance that the John Sheas and Antoine de Saint-Exupérys of our world will be reunited in the peace of belonging with their beloved whom they had come to know in the breaking of the bread on their wedding day. This will be the "rose-in-bloom time" of homecoming each of us longs for. Belonging has the last word because the Word was made flesh and dwelt amongst us! We each live for the return home.

# Notes

## Chapter One: *There Will Never Be Another You*

1. Eric Gill in Walter Kerr, *The Decline of Pleasure* (New York: Simon and Schuster, 1962), 202.

2. Albert Camus, "Letter to a German Friend," *Resistance, Rebellion and Death*, Justin McCarthy, tr. (New York: Knopf, 1961), 28.

3. Albert Camus, *The Plague*, Stuart Gilbert, tr. (New York: Random House, 1940), 278.

4. John Macmurray, *The Self as Agent* (London: Faber and Faber, 1957), 139–40.

5. Antoine de Saint-Exupéry, *Lettre à un Otage* (Paris: Gallimard, 1945), 19. Translation by Philip Mooney.

6. John Macmurray, *Religion, Art and Science* (Liverpool: Liverpool University Press, 1961), 25.

7. *Ibid.*

8. *Ibid.*, 24–25.

9. John Macmurray, *Reason and Emotion* (London: Faber and Faber, 1935), 156.

10. *Ibid.*, 151.

11. *Ibid.*, 188.

12. Kerr, *The Decline of Pleasure*, 13.

13. John Macmurray, *Persons in Relation* (London: Faber and Faber, 1961), 184.

14. Macmurray, *Reason and Emotion*, 156.

15. Macmurray, *Religion, Art and Science*, 38.

16. William V. Shannon, "The Network Circus," *The New York Times*, (September 3, 1977).

17. *Ibid.*

18. Neil Simon, "Tributes to Zero Mostel," *The New York Times* (September 18, 1977) II, 1.

19. Charles Augustus Lindbergh, *The Wartime Journals of Charles A. Lindbergh* (New York: Harcourt, Brace, Jovanovich, 1970), 241.

20. Antoine de Saint-Exupéry, *Flight to Arras*, Lewis Galantière, tr. (New York: Reynal and Hitchcock, 1942), 195.

21. Anne Morrow Lindbergh, "An Appreciation" in Antoine de Saint-Exupéry, *Wind, Sand and Stars*, Lewis Galantière, tr. (New York: Reynal and Hitchcock, 1939).

22. Antoine de Saint-Exupéry, *Wind, Sand and Stars*, Lewis Galantière, tr. (New York: Reynal and Hitchcock, 1939), 67.

23. *Ibid.*, 71.

24. Saint-Exupéry, *Flight to Arras*, 220.

25. Saint-Exupéry, *Wind, Sand and Stars*, 68.

26. Saint-Exupéry, *Flight to Arras*, 219.

27. *Ibid.*

## Chapter Two: *Value Images of the World*

1. Antoine de Saint-Exupéry, *The Little Prince*, Katherine Woods, tr. (New York: Harcourt, Brace, Jovanovich, 1971), 5–6.

2. *Ibid.* 94.

3. John Macmurray, *The Structure of Religious Experience* (London: Faber and Faber, 1936), 39.

4. Saint-Exupéry, *Lettre à un Otage*, 60.

5. William S. Gilbert, *Iolanthe*, Act II.

6. John Macmurray, *Freedom in the Modern World* (London: Faber and Faber, 1935), 173.

7. "Pastoral Constitution on the Church in the Modern World," *The Documents of Vatican II*, Walter M. Abbott, S.J., ed., Joseph Gallagher, dir. tr. (New York: America Press, 1966), 199–200.

8. Macmurray, *Freedom in the Modern World*, 188.

9. *Ibid.*, 188–89.

10. Saint-Exupéry, *Lettre à un Otage*, 62.

11. Macmurray, *Reason and Emotion*, 211.

12. Macmurray, *Freedom in the Modern World*, 148.

13. John Macmurray, "Prolegomena to a Christian Ethic," *Scottish Journal of Theology* IX, 1 (March 1956), 10.

14. Emmanuel Mounier, *Be Not Afraid*, Cynthia Rowland, tr. (New York: Sheed and Ward, 1962), 59.

15. *Ibid.*, 57.

16. Macmurray, *Reason and Emotion*, 47.

17. Saint-Exupéry, *The Little Prince*, 29.

18. See Bernard J.F. Lonergan, S.J., "The Absence of God in Modern Culture," *Presence and Absence of God: The Cardinal Bea Lectures*, Christopher F. Mooney, S.J., ed. (New York: Fordham University Press, 1969), 175. Regrettably, the graphic adjectival used by Lonergan in his live address is not in the published text.

19. Antoine de Saint-Exupéry, *Citadelle* (Paris: Gallimard, 1948), 205. Translation by Philip Mooney.

20. *Ibid.*, 45.

## Chapter Three: *The World of Friendship*

1. Saint-Exupéry, *The Little Prince*, 83.

2. Macmurray, *Persons in Relation*, 74.

3. Saint-Exupéry, *Lettre à un Otage*, 68–69.

4. John Macmurray, *Ye Are My Friends* (London: Friends Home Service Committee, 1964), 8.

5. Macmurray, *Persons in Relation*, 150.

6. Saint-Exupéry, *Citadelle*, 609.

7. John Macmurray, *Interpreting the Universe* (London: Faber and Faber, 1933), 136.

8. John Macmurray, *Conditions of Freedom* (London: Faber and Faber, 1950), 82.

9. Saint-Exupéry, *The Little Prince*, 31.

10. Saint-Exupéry, *Lettre à un Otage*, 68.

11. Macmurray, *Interpreting the Universe*, 137.

12. Saint-Exupéry, *The Little Prince*, 104.

13. *Ibid.*, 96.

14. Macmurray, *Reason and Emotion*, 255.

15. Macmurray, *Religion, Art and Science*, 66.

16. Saint-Exupéry, *The Little Prince*, 87.

17. Macmurray, *Persons in Relation*, 169–70.

18. Saint-Exupéry, *The Little Prince*, 87–88.

19. Saint-Exupéry, *Citadelle*, 235.

20. *Ibid.*, 562.

21. Macmurray, *Reason and Emotion*, 136.

22. *Ibid.*, 237.

23. *Ibid.*, 131.

24. Saint-Exupéry, *The Little Prince*, 93–94.

25. *Ibid.*, 104.

26. *Ibid*, 113.

27. Saint-Exupéry, *Lettre à un Otage*, 19.

28. Saint-Exupéry, *The Little Prince*, 106.

29. *Ibid.*, 11.

30. Saint-Exupéry, *Flight to Arras*, 56.

31. Saint-Exupéry, *The Little Prince*, 109.

32. Karl Rahner, S.J., *Theological Investigations IV*, Kevin Smyth, tr. (London: Darton, Longman and Todd, 1966), 120.

## Chapter Four: *Self-Protective Fear and Its Solution*

1. Macmurray, *Freedom in the Modern World*, 60.

2. See Saint-Exupéry, *Flight to Arras*, 243 and 247.

3. Macmurray, *Freedom in the Modern World*, 61.

4. John Macmurray, *To Save from Fear* (London: Friends Home Service Committee, 1964), 4.

5. Walter Kerr, *Tragedy and Comedy* (London: The Bodley Head, 1968), 294.

6. John Macmurray, *Creative Society* (New York: Association Press, 1936), 99.

7. W.J. Turner, *Mozart: The Man and His Works* (New York: Alfred A. Knopf, 1954), 283.

8. A. Alvarez in Martha Duffy, "Triumph of a Tormented Poet," *Life* LXXI (November 12, 1971), 38.

9. Saint-Exupéry, *Flight to Arras*, 203.

10. Saint-Exupéry, *Lettre à un Otage*, 19.

11. Arthur and Barbara Gelb, *O'Neill* (New York: Harper, 1960), 784.

12. Eugene O'Neill, *Days Without End* (New York: Random House, 1934), 44.

13. *Ibid.*, 156.

14. *Ibid.*

15. Gelb, *O'Neill*, 784.

16. *Ibid.*, 783–84.

17. O'Neill, *Days Without End*, 157.

18. Emmett Kelly with F. Beverly Kelly, *Clown* (New York: Prentice-Hall, 1954), 124.

19. *Ibid.*, 126.

20. Saint-Exupéry, *Wind, Sand and Stars*, 306.

21. See Matthew 1: 21.

22. O'Neill, *Days Without End*, 154.

## Chapter Five: *Prayer and Divine Presence*

1. See Samuel Howard Miller, "A Metaphor of the Self," *ARC Directions* 59 (Fall 1967), 1–5.

2. Macmurray, *Reason and Emotion*, 175.

3. Macmurray, *To Save from Fear*, 6.

4. Macmurray, *Reason and Emotion*, 65.

5. James Hilton, *Random Harvest* (Boston: Little, Brown, 1941), 286.

6. Ignatius Loyola in Maurice Giuliani, S.J., "Finding God in All Things," *Finding God in All Things*, William J. Young, S.J., tr., (Chicago: Henry Regnery, 1958), 20.

7. Fyodor M. Dostoyevsky, in André Malraux, *Felled Oaks*, Irene Clephane, tr. (New York: Holt, 1972), 36.

8. W. H. Auden, "Forgotten Prayer," *The New York Times* (February 2, 1971), I, 37.

9. Saint-Exupéry, *Citadelle*, 615.

10. *Ibid.*, 235.

11. John Macmurray, *Search for Reality in Religion* (London: Friends Home Service Committee, 1965), 53.

12. Karl Rahner and John Baptist Metz, *The Courage to Pray*, Sarah O'Brien Twohig, tr. (New York: Crossroad, 1981), 56.

13. Saint-Exupéry, *Lettre à un Otage*, 69.

## Chapter Six: *The Character of Love*

1. Macmurray, *Conditions of Freedom*, 79.

2. Macmurray, *Reason and Emotion*, 136, 137.

3. *Ibid.*, 141.

4. Saint-Exupéry, *Citadelle*, 188–89.

5. Macmurray, *Reason and Emotion*, 140–41.

6. Saint-Exupéry, *Citadelle*, 54.

7. *Ibid.*, 205.

8. Macmurray, *Reason and Emotion*, 206; cf. *Persons in Relation*, 159.

9. Macmurray, *Persons in Relation*, 159.

10. Ian D. Suttie, *The Origins of Love and Hate* (New York: Julian Press, 1935), 23.

11. Macmurray, *Persons in Relation*, 73.

12. John Macmurray, *The Clue to History* (London: Harper, 1938), 194.

13. Macmurray, *Persons in Relation*, 74.

14. See Matthew 23: 23

15. Macmurray, *The Structure of Religious Experience*, 46.

16. Gerard Manley Hopkins, "Spring and Fall: To a Child," *Poems of Gerard Manley Hopkins* (London: Oxford University Press, 1948), 94.

## Chapter Seven: *Love in Action*

1. Macmurray, *Reason and Emotion*, 222.

2. Macmurray, *Self as Agent*, 15.

3. Thomas Moore, "Songs from M. P.; or, The Blue Stocking."

4. *Fred Allen's Letters*, Joe McCarthy, ed. (New York: Doubleday, 1966), 316.

5. Walter Kerr, *Thirty Plays Hath November* (New York, 1969), 114.

6. Macmurray, *Reason and Emotion*, 125, 126.

*Notes*

7. Geoffrey Chaucer, *Tale of the Man of Law*, II(B).1/ 1075.

8. Saint-Exupéry, *The Little Prince*, 87.

9. "Pastoral Constitution," II, 1, No. 48 and 49, 250-53.

10. Macmurray, *Reason and Emotion*, 256.

11. Harold Pinter, *Betrayal* (New York: Grove Press, 1978), 136.

12. Macmurray, *Reason and Emotion*, 137-38.

13. Saint-Exupéry, *Wind, Sand and Stars*, 306.

14. Macmurray, *Freedom in the Modern World*, 218.

## Chapter Eight: *The Celebration of Belonging*

1. François Mauriac, *De Gaulle*, Richard Howard, tr. (New York: Doubleday, 1966), 5.

2. William Butler Yeats, *Plays and Controversies* (New York: Macmillan, 1924), 131.

3. William Butler Yeats, "The Lover Tells of the Rose in His Heart," *The Collected Poems of W.B. Yeats* (New York: Macmillan, 1956), 54.

4. Saint-Exupéry, *Lettre à un Otage*, 69.

5. Anne Morrow Lindbergh, *Gift from the Sea* (New York: Pantheon Books, 1955), 104.

6. Saint-Exupéry, *Citadelle*, 58-59.

7. Saint-Exupéry, *Flight to Arras*, 209.

8. *Ibid.*, 217-18.

9. John Macmurray, *A Challenge to the Churches* (London: Keegan Paul, 1941), 25.

10. Macmurray, *Reason and Emotion*, 65.

11. Saint-Exupéry, *Lettre à un Otage*, 41.

# Bibliography

## Books

Allen, Fred. *Fred Allen's Letters*. Joe McCarthy, ed. New York: Doubleday, 1966.

Camus, Albert. "Letter to a German Friend," *Resistance, Rebellion and Death*. Justin McCarthy, trans. New York: Alfred A. Knopf, 1961.

———. *The Plague*. Stuart Gilbert, trans. New York: Random House, 1940.

Gelb, Arthur and Barbara. *O'Neill*. New York: Harper, 1960.

Giuliani, Maurice, S.J. *Finding God in All Things*. William J. Young, trans. Chicago: Henry Regnery, 1958.

Hilton, James. *Random Harvest*. Boston: Little, Brown, 1941.

Hopkins, Gerard Manley. *Collected Poems*. London: Oxford University Press, 1967.

Kelly, Emmett. *Clown*. New York: Prentice-Hall, 1954.

Kerr, Walter. *The Decline of Pleasure*. New York: Simon and Schuster, 1962.

———. *Tragedy and Comedy*. London: The Bodley Head, 1968.

Lindbergh, Anne Morrow. *Gift from the Sea*. New York: Pantheon Books, 1955.

Lindbergh, Charles Augustus. *The Wartime Journals of Charles A. Lindberg.* New York: Harcourt, Brace, Jovanovich, 1970.

Macmurray, John. *A Challenge to the Churches.* London: Keegan Paul, 1941.

————. *The Clue to History.* London: Harper, 1939.

————. *Conditions of Freedom.* London: Faber and Faber, 1950.

————. *Creative Society.* New York: Association Press, 1936.

————. *Freedom in the Modern World.* London: Faber and Faber, 1935.

————. *Interpreting the Universe.* London: Faber and Faber, 1933.

————. *Persons in Relation.* London: Faber and Faber, 1961.

————. *Reason and Emotion.* London: Faber and Faber, 1935.

————. *Religion, Art and Science.* Liverpool: Liverpool University Press, 1961.

————. *Search for Reality in Religion.* London: Friends Home Service Committee, 1965.

————. *The Self as Agent.* London: Faber and Faber, 1957.

————. *The Structure of Religious Experience.* London: Faber and Faber, 1936.

Malraux, André. *Felled Oaks.* Irene Clephane, tr. New York: Holt, 1972.

Mauriac, François. *De Gaulle.* Richard Howard, trans. New York: Doubleday, 1966.

Mounier, Emmanuel. *Be Not Afraid.* Cynthia Rowland, trans. New York: Sheed and Ward, 1962.

O'Neill, Eugene G. *Days Without End.* New York: Random House, 1934.

Pinter, Harold. *Betrayal.* New York: Grove Press, 1978.

Rahner, Karl, S.J. *Theological Investigations IV.* Kevin Smith, trans., London: Darton, Longman and Todd, 1966.

Rahner, Karl, and Metz, John Baptist. *The Courage To Pray.* Sarah O'Brien Twohig, trans. New York: Crossroad, 1981.

Saint-Exupéry, Antoine de. *Citadelle.* Paris: Gallimard, 1948.

————. *Flight to Arras.* Lewis Galantière, trans. New York: Reynal and Hitchcock, 1942.

————. *Lettre à un Otage.* Paris: Gallimard, 1945.

————. *The Little Prince.* Katherine Woods, trans. New York: Harcourt, Brace, Jovanovich, 1971.

_____. *Wind, Sand and Stars.* Lewis Galantière, trans. New York: Reynal and Hitchcock, 1939.

Suttie, Ian D. *The Origins of Love and Hate.* New York: Julian Press, 1935.

Turner, W. J. *Mozart: The Man and His Works.* New York: Alfred A. Knopf, 1924.

Yeats, William Butler. *Plays and Controversies.* New York: Macmillan, 1956.

_____. *Collected Poems of W. B. Yeats.* New York: Macmillan, 1956.


## Collections

*Presence and Absence of God: The Cardinal Bea Lectures.* Christopher F. Mooney, S.J., ed. New York: Fordham University Press, 1969.

*The Documents of Vatican II.* Walter M. Abbott, S.J., ed. New York: America Press, 1966.


## Pamphlets

Macmurray, John. *To Save from Fear.* London: Friends Home Service Committee, 1964.

_____. *Ye Are My Friends.* London, Friends Home Service Committee, 1964.


## Articles

Auden, W. H., "Forgotten Prayer," *The New York Times*, February 2, 1971.

Duffy, Martha. "Triumph of a Tormented Poet," *Life*, LXXI: November 12, 1971.

Macmurray, John. "Prolegomena to a Christian Ethic," *Scottish Journal of Theology* IX, 1: March 1956.

Miller, Samuel Howard. "A Metaphor of the Self," *ARC Directions 59. New York: Foundations for the Arts, Religion and Culture*, Fall 1967.

Shannon, William V. "The Network Circus," *The New York Times*, September 3, 1977.

Simon, Neil. "Tributes to Zero Mostel," *The New York Times*, September 18, 1977.